DEFINING YOUR SUCCESS FACTORS

A COLLECTION OF BRIEF TALKS ON THE CRITICAL SUCCESS FACTORS IN YOUR LIFE THAT WILL HELP YOU ACCOMPLISH YOUR GOALS AND THRIVE IN LIFE.

DR. AMIT DAS

To

All my bosses, associates, and students who made a difference in my professional career.

"Success is the state of having attained a goal or objective, which is the opposite of failure. Make sure you are aware of what success, achievement, and wealth in general mean to you personally. There is no universal definition of success since everyone has a unique perspective on what it means to live prosperously and defines success differently. While some people may view possessing expensive cars, travelling abroad, career growth, good increments, and a large home as the ultimate definition of success, others see it as leading a life filled with love and happiness with their family. Both are correct. "

- Dr. Amit Das, Motivational Speaker, Leadership Coach and Mentor.

Contents

Thoughts *vii*

Foreword *ix*

Preface *xv*

Acknowledgements *xix*

1. Your Mental Clarity Regarding Success 1
2. Your Mental Toughness Predicts Success 5
3. Your Winning Attitude Decides Sustainability 10
4. Your Determination Gives Unwavering Strength 15
5. Your Limitation Is Your Imagination 19
6. Your Self-belief Influences Your Success 25
7. Your Disability Is Not A Liability 35
8. Your Failure Is Not Final 43
9. Your Hard Work Is Crucial To Your Success 51
10. Your Willpower Outweigh All Challenges 62
11. Your Bigger Dreams Are Driven By Your Passion 73
12. Your Success Is Transient, Evanescent 85

References 97

About The Author 99

Thoughts

"Your Success"
"If you put up the effort,
you can succeed and develop your skills.
You're prepared now for whatever chgallenges,
you accept your focus on deals.
You have tremendous power, indispensable energy
you have set goals to accomplish.
Your heart is celebrating your progress
do they appreciate or are purely selfish?
You may lose or squander the day
with a thoughless inner drive,
You bravely turn to the future
once you get positive vibes.
Your key to happiness neither dwells
in the realm of feeble desires,
rather, in your proactive preparation
and it comes from your within fires.
You work with misery or joy
your choice in reaching your destination,
you have a winning attitude
your dreams are driven by your passion.
Your transient setback and roadblocks
your utter failure and temporal pain,
life question your ability
it's a game without loss no gain.
Change your mindset; change your thoughts,
accentuate the affirmation.
a single triumph does not guarantee success
requires high aims and focus need in combination."
By
-Dr. Amit Das, Motivational Speaker, Leadership Coach, and Mentor.

Foreword

"Success is not final, failure is not fatal: it is the courage to continue that counts"- Winston Churchill

You can achieve anything you can dream of!

Dear Readers,

Thank you for taking the time to learn more about your defining success factors and the rewarding outcome of increasing your personal productivity. The only way you think will define how successful you are, regardless of where you are from, how educated you are, or the situations you find yourself in. This book will make you question your ability to overcome obstacles, achieve your goals, and have a fulfilling life. You'll realise what all really successful individuals have in common after reading this book.

"Defining Your Success Factors " is a must have, regardless of your level of experience with personal development or how long you've been using success concepts. It is jam-packed with important basic ideas that anybody can use to improve their quality of life, presented in engrossing bits of knowledge. Additionally, the author has a system of internal assistance to guarantee your success.

Dr. Amit Das, a motivational speaker, mentor, counsellor, and coach, will demonstrate how to take charge and unlock your latent potential via effective methods, regardless of your viewpoint being negative, positive, or somewhere in between.

This book, which is extremely encouraging and inspirational, wants its readers to realise that a sunrise and a beautiful day always follow a long and gloomy night. Despite repeated failures, the author exhorts his readers to never give up since there is always a way out of any challenging circumstance. He discusses a variety of stressful scenarios that people encounter on a regular basis. such as long-term illness, losing a loved one, being unemployed, and other frightful circumstances that might obstruct a person's path to achievement. The author provides his readers with a variety of guidelines to help them deal with all of these challenges.

There is a fix for each issue. The chance of resolving the issue also arises when you discuss it someplace. He offers simple procedures that may be used to assess the feasibility of novel concepts. In this book, he has also included guidelines and strategies to prevent burnout. The wonderful part about all the concepts discussed in "Defining Your Success Factors" is that they are written and presented in such a way that they can be applied to nearly any circumstance.

Even better, you'll have a personal insight into how you really compare and what needs to change in you in order to alter the trajectory of your personal life. This book is a collection of brief talks on your life's critical factors to accomplishing your pursuits and thriving in life. Through this book, you will learn from top achievers, established leaders, and individuals how they have excelled in their lives. With the appropriate balance of your thoughts, speech, and actions, you may strengthen the version of yourself that brings you joy and success. The author has used a distinctive literary technique to create and communicate a message about success that is sure to be memorable and life-changing. This book outlines the essential success criteria that are truly important if you want to experience exceptional success in life.

You'll find a summary of the ideas and lessons contained in the greatest literature in this book. This book is for everyone who wants to learn how to improve their quality of life generally and have greater success in their lives. Read the book to find out more about how a fresh look at core ideas may help you succeed in both your personal and professional life. This book has the following benefits: understanding key concepts; acquiring actionable ideas and key takeaways; and expanding your knowledge and succeeding in your life.

By teaching you how to strive, understand, create, condition, envision, and savour, this book demonstrates how to find your life's purpose and then begin living it. The book is written in straightforward terms for the average reader; it is not a place for jargon or mysticism. It gives you options so you can go your own way, believe in your progress, and be confident enough to move forward.and after that. Your own dreams are the key; all you need is this book.

The secret to one's own success is given in the book. It does not require the buzz of an euphoric "high" to motivate you. The author encourages you to put yourself first in your life and provides you with the chance to read and reflect. The author shows you how to use such understated yet really powerful notions as "detachment" and "plenty" in your life by subtly luring the reader to think about them.

The author of the book provides you with techniques to train your mindset so that you can protect against negative ideas and cultivate the habit of positive thinking. It will show you how to develop positive thinking that will enable you to realise your full potential. You will achieve beyond your wildest expectations thanks to it.

However, the author goes to great efforts to explain how the brain functions in a psychological environment and how this information may be applied to enhance your quality of life. In order to bridge the gap between emotional intelligence and self-development, the book takes you on an engaging and educational journey.

You can do this by using the motivational self-help book. Anyone who reads it will benefit personally and psychologically from it. Dr. Amit Das discusses actions you can take to create a fulfilling, flourishing life, including: spending an hour in silence to develop your creative vision; going above and beyond to help others; letting your strengths guide your work; reflecting on your mistakes; learning to manage your time effectively; and much more. The book “Defining Your Success Factors” strives to set you free from the bonds of your shackling ideas so that you may overcome your restraints and let your souls soar.

Each of these topics has unspoken, crucial success characteristics that successful individuals know how to use. The urge to consistently raise the value you provide to the organisation you work for is the one thing that unites everyone's career. There are multiple lessons on the determinants of success in this workbook. This brief study aims to assist you in identifying and fostering each of these success characteristics in your own personal life so that you may start to advance and win over people.

The author is renowned for his ability to reduce difficult subjects to straightforward actions that can be used in both daily life and the workplace. Here, he pulls on the best research in stress management, human behaviour, life, and psychology to produce an approachable manual for using effective planning to make good habits inescapable and bad habits unavoidable.

The author uses inspiring tales of how authors, artists, entrepreneurs, and innovators have harnessed this capacity to achieve the highest of heights to demonstrate his ideas. The book has proven to be quite inspirational and has helped many readers overcome poor self-esteem and accomplish their own goals. The author outlines many strategies for overcoming setbacks and difficulties while remaining true to one's principles and utilising only just methods to achieve it. This book will inspire you to create more precise goals, become a mind-master today, and accomplish any objectives you set for yourself. This book offers tried-and-true methods for developing self-control so you may transform your life and accomplish any objective you set for yourself.

"Success is no accident. It is hard work, perseverance, learning, studying, sacrifice and most of all, love of what you are doing or learning to do."- Pele

Thank you for taking the time to read this book.

So, happy reading and learning to all my readers.

Carpe diem.

Dr. Amit Das

Motivational Speaker, Leadership Coach, and Mentor.

Preface

"Success does not mean an absence of problems, it is overcoming problems. Success is not measured by how high we go up in life, but how many times we bounce back when we fall down." — Shiv Khera

Do you believe that you are not successful and that only others are?

Your definition of success could contain more of one than the other, or it might be a combination of the two. It may potentially be something completely different. No matter how you currently define success, this short but mighty book called "Defining Your Success Factors " will undoubtedly change the way you think about and define it. This includes a wide range of remarkable stories and examples. The message will strike a chord with you deeply and leave you feeling deeply responsible for how you decide to accomplish the success you want. These include initiative, enthusiasm, optimism, decision-making, using failure to your advantage, selecting heroes carefully, managing oneself, managing one's boss, managing others, and leading others.

The majority of success books are filled with complex ideas that are challenging for most people to comprehend and use in their daily lives. You can do a miracle for yourself. From where you are right now, it will lead you to attain everything you desire in life. It is jam-packed with real-world examples and the essential success principles that you can quickly apply to change your life. The success of the book as a whole You only need your self-miracle and the desire to transform. This book is ideal for readers who are short on time or who want a thorough knowledge of the fundamentals and lessons of important business and life skills. In the context of success, I examine a range of subjects, including goal-setting, love, change, fear, and concern. A multitude of ideas, counsel, and strategies are shared to assist you in overcoming unconscious restrictions and unlocking your full brilliance.

This book primarily discusses the fundamental mental skills required as a basis for the reader to construct a successful, happy, and fulfilling life. If you approach the book with this in mind, you may rapidly see how the recommendations presented can help you become the person you really want to be and get personally connected with them. This book will hold your hand as you embark on this incredible adventure of self-transformation and self-growth, and personality development is a trip worth taking. This book is with real-life quotes from business leaders from all walks of life who used the science of 30 minutes of successful planning to perfect their trade and rise to the top of their profession will inspire and amuse readers along the way. Even when life gets wilder, even crazier, learn how to develop fresh and correct plans in as little as 30 minutes.

- ***Are you afraid to go to work?***
- ***Do you feel worn out, depressed, or burdened down?***
- ***Have you abandoned your aspirations?***

Everyone aspires to have a more successful life, but sadly, very few people know how to take the necessary measures to get there. The good news is that, regardless of your exact objectives, if you use everything you're going to learn in this book, you will succeed in every aspect of your life.

Success and achievement are not the same things, despite the fact that accomplishment is sometimes connected with success. When you try to achieve particular goals, you call it an accomplishment when you get the desired results. In essence, it refers to the outcomes you anticipate or plan for. Success is the result or benefit of a goal that has been attained. The meaning of achievement with each objective you complete, you move closer to financial security and a prosperous life. Through this book, you will learn from top achievers, established leaders, and individuals who have excelled in their fields. Every day, read just one definition and one chapter. Think about it, eat it up, and accept it. Own it. Allow the revelations to permeate your spirit and give you the insight, drive, and inspiration you need to release the genuinely exceptional performance that is inside you.

- ***Do you intend to make significant changes in your life?***
- ***Have you attempted to change but ended up reverting to your previous behaviour?***
- ***Have you tried to form a habit but been unsuccessful?***

Most likely, since you're reading this, you do. It's not just you. In clarity, the only piece in a range of pieces where spirituality navigates the landscape shaped by the human mind's wanderings is the book's straightforward writing and transparent presentation tackle contentious spirituality-related issues with a certain sense of newness that will excite the mind and drive one to reconsider and relearn. The author demonstrates how to lower stress, sharpen attention, unleash extraordinary creativity, increase productivity exponentially, and restore equilibrium based on the crucial idea that winning begins at the start of the day. Your life may undergo a life-changing makeover in as little as 30 minutes every day. Be deliberate. Be inspired.

"People who succeed have momentum. The more they succeed, the more they want to succeed, and the more they find a way to succeed. Similarly, when someone is failing, the tendency is to get on a downward spiral that can even become a self-fulfilling prophecy."- Tony Robbins

You can now choose. Clicking the order button now can either transform your life for the better or worse for the foreseeable future compared to doing nothing.

Acknowledgements

At the outset, I will thank my family for supporting me throughout the journey of writing my book and encouraging me to live my dreams; my son has always been instrumental in giving his inspiration to complete the writing of this book. Despite the fact that I am listed as the author of this book, "Defining Your Success Factors" would not have been published if I had depended entirely on my own talents. Creating this book required more than anything—it took a family of dedicated and caring people who were always prepared to lend a hand.

Writing a book while working full-time is no simple task, so I'd want to express my gratitude to my amazing coworkers who act as cheerleaders in equal measure. Thank you, too, to my students and clients for your patience and unflinching support while I worked on this book!

Thank you to everyone who has listened to me argue for doing everything you can to make your life, including your work life, more progressive. I appreciate everyone's assistance throughout the process. This book would not have been possible without each of you having had an impact on my life in some manner.

Lastly, I would like to thank all the people with whom I have been associated. You gave me power. I would like to thank Notion Press for publishing my book. Finally, thank you all for gifting your time to read this book.

I'd want to convey my heartfelt appreciation to the almighty God for bestowing his blessings and being so gracious.

CHAPTER ONE

Your Mental Clarity Regarding Success

"Try not to become a man of success, but rather try to become a man of value." - Albert Einstein

The mind is where success begins.

What does "success" mean to you? Is it your income or your investments that matter? Is it the size of each, or the price you paid for your house or car? Is it your track record for promotions or your reputation in the neighbourhood? Is it that you've accomplished more than you ever thought possible or that you've triumphed over really difficult situations that nobody would have believed feasible? Perhaps you think that your success depends on the possessions you have. On the other hand, you can believe that success is dependent on intangible factors like connections like love or friendship.

How will you defining success?
What it means?

How to define success, which most people can't do and frequently have greater difficulty accomplishing their objectives because they're unsure of what success looks like for them. You may achieve success in life if you are given the appropriate direction. Success is the state of having attained a goal or objective, which is the opposite of failure. The accomplishment of intended visions and deliberated goals defines success. Success may also refer to a certain social standing that designates an affluent individual who may also have achieved notoriety for a successful conclusion.

What does "success in life" mean?

You are the only one who can provide a response to the above query. Since this is not conceivable, I am neither able nor prepared to offer a definitive definition of success. There is no universal definition of success since everyone has a unique perspective on what it means to live prosperously and defines success differently. It's crucial that you understand exactly what constitutes success in life. Make sure you are aware of what success, achievement, and wealth in general mean to you personally.

> "*While some people may view possessing expensive automobiles and a large home as the ultimate definition of success, others see it as leading a life filled with love and happiness with their family.*"

You may focus on your ambitions and goals once you have determined what is essential to you individually. The definition of success knowing what success means in your own personal life is one of the most crucial first stages to success in life. The definitions of success that are most commonly used, such as having a lot of money, being affluent, possessing many material possessions, and having degrees, are far from the genuine definition of success.

Where do the brightest minds in the world receive their inspiration?

Excellent books! Everyone is curious about what it takes to achieve long-lasting success in both business and life. It all boils down to having a firm understanding of the principles of business and life skills, the same ones that successful people are taught at many of the most prominent schools in the world, together with useful life lessons.

As you read the book, it will subtly assist you in finding personal happiness in your own way, which is always the best course of action for you. With the help of this book for the twenty-first century, you'll be able to handle whatever society throws at you and succeed in life.

How can one be successful in life?

Elaborate goal setting is the first step in the journey of success. Define your approach and plan for achieving your objectives, aspirations, and visions. Remember that success is the result of a string of achievements, so be careful to break down your goals into more manageable subgoals.

One of the most well-known modern authorities on achievement, inspiration, and living a balanced life was the late Zig Ziglar. In his book Born to Win!, he makes the case that success cannot be summed up in a single phrase but rather is made up of a variety of factors. One may counter that each person's definition is unique and that no one definition fits everyone. Each of us has a different definition of success. For some, it could entail achieving popularity or a specific level of social standing, while for others, it just means being really content and happy no matter what.

The number of individuals who can live better, more evolved lives as a result of what you developed is a stronger indicator of actual success than any of the aforementioned metrics. This is what success means. Not the medals others spend their lifetimes accumulating. You are frequently led to believe by the media and society that having a prosperous life entails having a lot of material possessions. Success, however, is defined as leading a happy life and improving the quality of life for everyone on this planet. Is having a flashy sports vehicle the true mark of success? The meaning of failure is the reverse of success since it refers to failing when attempting to accomplish goals or objectives.

Never attempt to post a successful formula. When you use yourself to the fullest, you achieve real success. Success implies that you are enjoying your life to the fullest extent possible, regardless of whether you want to become a doctor, a politician, a yogi, or anything else. You require perception and active intellect if that needs to happen. You have the essential intellect to live life well if you can perceive it for what it is. Your intelligence will work against you if you are unable to accept life as it is. In our world, intelligent people tend to be the most unhappy individuals. They just do not see life, although they have an active mind.

In addition to the conventional understanding of failure, it is also true that even affluent and successful people experience failure in their lives. Just consider all the scandals, addictions, and suicides involving the affluent and famous. All of them were amazing people, but many of them were also profoundly dissatisfied with their lives and unable to comprehend what success really meant. The qualities in your life that make you a happy person, such as friendship, connections, and your family, rather than money, are what define wealth.

People who are afraid to try and those who are concerned that you will succeed are the two groups of people who will tell you that you cannot change the world. Successful individuals are prepared to take risks that failed people are not. Instead of wishing it were simpler, strive to improve. Keep in mind that success often seems to be linked to action. Successful individuals never stand still. They make errors, but they keep going.

"There are two types of people who will tell you that you cannot make a difference in this world: those who are afraid to try and those who are afraid you will succeed."- Ray Goforth

CHAPTER TWO

Your Mental Toughness Predicts Success

"The scope of one's personality is defined by the magnitude of that problem which is capable of driving a person out of his wits."
— Sigmund Freud

How to use your mind's abilities to solve any difficulty!

This chapter provides a comprehensive explanation of this amazing power of mental strength. These are the mindset, skills, and habits that must be developed if you want to become invincible. These parts were chosen based on the author's research over the previous ten years and his work with a variety of people, including students, senior professionals, and celebrities.

It's a common proverb: how we react to events is far more important to our happiness and success than how they affect us. Keep your thoughts and self-talk positive and avoid the habits that lead to negativity and bad behaviour if you want to develop and sustain the type of mental fortitude that success demands. The people who win conflicts we never see them fight are the strongest, not those who display power in front of us.

> *"Practice and awareness are necessary to develop a strong mental capacity. It necessitates being aware of your poor behaviours and making an effort to develop new ones to take their place."*

Perhaps not many, but Smt. Draupadi Murmu, our 15th nation's president, has been through many catastrophes, including the loss of her husband and two of her sons. News sources state that one of her sons departed tragically in 2009 under strange circumstances, and that her second son perished in a car accident three years later. She had already lost her husband to cardiac arrest. Smt. Murmu reportedly experienced sadness and anxiety at one point, but she made the decision to rise above her personal setbacks and commit her life to social change and public service. Smt. Murmu sought solace from her misery by joining the BrahmKumari community and travelling the spiritual path.

> *"If you want to succeed, intelligence might be useful, but you also need to have dedication and mental toughness. Maintain your focus with these helpful behaviours."*

Smt. Draupadi Murmu is familiar with the harsh realities of life and the battle for existence faced by the average person. She has faced adversity in her life, but she has persevered by walking the public way without complaint. She overcame several obstacles to get her education despite being born into an average household. Smt. Draupadi Murmu is a representation of the strong Indian woman who overcomes numerous obstacles in life. Her fight against hardships and personal tragedies has been continuous and protracted. She overcame them and added adventure to her life. She has experience working in state secretariats; serving two terms in the legislature; serving as a minister in Odisha; and serving as an effective governor in a state with a predominance of tribalism. Smt. Draupadi Murmu's election as India's president will greatly advance women's rights. This is an occasion to congratulate Smt.

Draupadi Murmu, who has been elected as our nation's second female president and first tribal woman. Being elected president, she represents the genuine beauty of her inspirational life path, which was filled with highs and lows, tragedies, and losses.

"Always be yourself and have faith in yourself. Do not go out and look for a successful personality and try to duplicate it." -- Bruce Lee

Dr. APJ Abdul Kalam, known as the Missile Man of India, is highly regarded throughout the globe. He was a brilliant scientist, educator, and president of the people. He led a straightforward, modest life, giving his all to his career and the country. He made significant contributions to the development of missiles and was the 11th President of India.

> *"No matter how much time and effort we put into achieving a goal, life does not always go according to our plan. There will be moments when it takes a different direction and forces you to follow it. Next, what? It is crucial to be ready in these situations."*

You need to be in the appropriate frame of mind to choose the next course of action that will ensure you get back on track. He emphasised that you need to conquer your fear and take charge of the issue if you want to stand out. The ideal strategy for success is to treat both victory and failure with equal stoicism. Both go together seamlessly. If you can learn to accept failure, you'll start to focus more on the problem's solution than its root cause. You will be astounded to discover how you can perfect the skill of succeeding if you learn to approach your failures the same way you treat success.

He underlined that his mission was to have the guts to think creatively, to create, to forge new paths, to find solutions to difficulties, and to achieve. This was especially true for young people. What are your chances of passing in a country like ours when thousands of students are studying and vying for that one spot in their ideal college? The key factor in this situation is not the amount of time you spend solving a paper, but rather your intellect and thinking! Dare to think differently and choose a strategy that makes you stand out from the crowd.

> *"To live a successful life, vision and planning are both essential. Whichever happens first? Definitely a vision. Having a distinct vision in mind can help you choose the best course of action."*

If your vision is unclear, no approach will succeed for you. Continue on after that! Once a vision has been established in your mind, nurture it, make progress toward it, watch for when it comes to pass, and then prepare to benefit from it. This should be at the top of the list because, without it, everything else falls short. Dr. Kalam constantly emphasised that even as the leader of a whole country, you should never lose sight of your modest nature.

It is crucial to constantly preserve humility and a sense of reality no matter where life leads you. Because humility triumphs where egoism fails, it has always been a desirable quality. Everyone respects the great scientist for his beliefs, brilliance, and simplicity. He was the driving force behind India's development as a major nuclear power on the globe.

> *"According to Dr. Kalam, to ensure that your dreams come true, you must first have dreams and see dreams. Even though a dream seems unachievable, you may still make it come true by dreaming it."*

A generation of young Indians was inspired by the former Indian President's speeches and accomplishments. He claims that you need to adopt a different way of thinking and have the courage to venture through uncharted territory, come up with novel ideas, and learn how the seemingly impossible may be accomplished. He was of the opinion that facing challenges requires guts. Dr. Kalam had a lot of trust in Indians and wished for their countrymen and women to devote themselves completely to their objectives. He thought that the secret to success was commitment. The eminent scientist argued that having a dream is the first step. Be courageous and open to new ideas. You must have the guts to think differently, that is the important truths about life.

In order to help his family, who hailed from a low-income background, Dr. Abdul Kalam used to hand out newspapers after school. He was respected for his sharp intelligence and diligence, even though he was never the top student at his school. He stood out from the other pupils because of his intense desire to master mathematics. He showed us that, with patience, dreams can come true. He also taught us not to be afraid of goals and deadlines.

Dr. Kalam was given the nickname "Missile Man" for his tireless efforts in the development of ballistic missiles. It is true that a person's worth is determined by how hard he works and how sincerely he tries. He has received multiple honorary doctorates from more than 40 universities throughout the world. The secret to development and evolution is education. It's crucial to always learn from life. Despite his achievements, Dr. Dr. Kalam was one of the most likeable presidents due to his generosity, compassion, and unwavering love for everyone. Dr. Kalam never sought out any positions or sought to be in the spotlight. He used to devote himself fully to his work, and despite never asking for any of the positions, they all came his way.

"To the person making them up, excuses sound great. But justifications have no place in life. There is not much time left in life. You can't hold on even though it will go on forever. And believe that each day is a gift. A pledge to pursue your dreams! Nobody is aware of the nature of your dream. No one is concerned about how discouraging it may have been for you to strive for your goal. However, the fantasy you're keeping in your head is conceivable. Life takes on a new kind of significance when you run in the direction of your dreams."- Dr. APJ Abdul Kalam

CHAPTER THREE

Your Winning Attitude Decides Sustainability

"Champions aren't made in the gyms. Champions are made from something they have deep inside them-a desire, a dream, a vision."
- Muhammad Ali

Your future may be altered by your attitude.

All of us desire greater success in one or more areas of our lives. Maybe you'd want to have a more fulfilling profession, a closer and more passionate love life, to purchase the home of your dreams, or to have a bigger good effect on the world. Whatever success means to you, it is attainable with the winning attitude.

Having a good attitude involves more than simply having a grin on your face. It involves keeping a positive outlook and attitude even while everything around you is in complete disarray. Positive and negative ideas are considered to have a similar effect on your mind as a healthy or unhealthy diet has on your physical health. Positive ideas will help you witness great improvements in the world around you.

> "*Your attitude sets the tone for a better, more prosperous life, and you have power over it.*"

When you begin to think positively, your mind gets free of any negative ideas, and you begin to perceive the world in a new way. You will no longer blame yourself or other people. You will have complete emotional control and make an effort to learn something from every setback you encounter. It is well known that happiness and a good outlook go hand in hand. Happiness is a mental state that originates from the inside and is not reliant on outside circumstances. Positive thinking will bring harmony and happiness into your life. Simply said, no matter what circumstances you are in, you may be happy right now if you have a positive mindset.

> "*Those who have a positive outlook on life are vivacious, active, and healthy.*"

Positive thinking has a beneficial impact on your health as well, reducing stress and enhancing your general welfare. Even when you are sick, your body heals more quickly. By adopting a positive outlook, you can establish emotional equilibrium, which really aids the brain's healthy operation. You develop the ability to maintain attention, which enables you to make wise choices in difficult circumstances. You'll start to feel better about yourself after you adopt an optimistic outlook. Your confidence and inner strength will increase as a result of treating yourself with more love and respect. You'll overcome your self-limiting beliefs and take on fresh tasks.

> "*You could approach a challenge with a lot of excitement, but should you keep going if no progress is being made? Most individuals give up because they perceive it to be too difficult.*"

Here is an inspiring story of a winning attitude that changed the rules of success for you. Yes, I am referring to Karoly Takacs, one of my all-time favourite characters, who lost his primary shooting hand due to the explosion of a grenade at an army camp. Karoly

Takacs served in the Hungarian armed forces. Around 1936, Karoly Takacs had already established himself as the world's top pistol shooter. He spent more than a year in hospital by himself and kept a low profile for a month after he was discharged from the hospital. The Hungarian National Pistol Championship was held in the spring of 1939. When the other shooters noticed Karoly Takacs had come, they commiserated with him at his loss and expressed their pleasure in seeing him attend the event.

Although the explosion did not kill him, it severely wounded his right hand, his shooting hand, rendering it useless for the rest of his life. He was heartbroken by the loss of both his right hand and the chance to compete for a gold medal at the top level of the sport. To everyone's amazement, Takacs said he wasn't there to watch but rather to take part. Everyone anticipated Takacs would attempt to weakly pull the trigger with his right hand at the start of the event to slake his emotional craving for another shot. Takacs, on the other hand, grabbed the gun with his left hand when it was his time. The spectators stared in disbelief as he fired shot after shot with his non-dominant hand. And what was astonishing was that each shot found its target. Takacs was declared the event's victor.

He reasoned, "Why should I be concerned about the right hand I don't have?" Let me try using my left hand to see what I can achieve. There it was. After hard practise and perseverance over several months, he was able to play again. But his hopes of taking home Olympic gold were once more dashed. This time around, owing to the World War II-related cancellation of the 1940 Olympics by the Olympic Committee. et it took him until 1948—only 12 years!—to capture the Olympic gold medal.

Only those with strong mental fortitude will be able to get past a traumatic experience, pick themselves up again, and resume performing at a world-class level. The majority of shooters would not have even bothered to attempt using their left hand. Takacs did not, however. He took no blame, returned to practise, and made a great recovery. Every person encounters problems. When they occur, you can choose to put the blame on external factors or look for ways to make improvements. If you want to, you can always come up with an explanation for why things went wrong.

The simplest way to ignore your own faults or stay in your comfort zones is to blame other factors. You could be angry with the government for the weak economy, with society for having dirty streets, and with your job for giving you a low-quality raise. Yet you fail to make greater use of what you already have. Put an end to your concern about what the rest of the world does or does not do for you.

> "*Do not depend on others to assist you in achieving success in life. You are a power and your own master. Pay attention to what you have and work on yourself.*"

For instance, you are unable to do anything to prevent delays brought on by bad weather or traffic. You have limited control when the government alters the tax system in a way that affects your profits. If a natural disaster makes headlines, thinking about it will only make your mood worse. There are things that both you and I can modify and have some influence over, as well as those that we have no control over at all. We are believed to have a locus of control over the regions that we can affect. Concerns about factors beyond their control cause people to become nervous and agitated.

You develop, mature, change, and gain experience via failing. You are aware of what doesn't work, potential trouble spots, and downward spirals. With a clear picture of everything in your head, you can better prepare yourself and feel more confident and self-assured. Your vision of the difficulties and hurdles changes as a result of your faith. Every "no" indicates you need to find another route, and every "barrier" means you need to find a different route. Failure in no way entails packing it up and walking away. This optimistic perspective completely transforms your life and raises you to the rank of a champion. When you have a winning attitude, you become unstoppable and motivated to pursue goals that other people would consider unachievable."

"None of us have it easy in life. What, then, is that? We need to be persistent and, most importantly, confident in ourselves. We have to think that we have a talent for something, and that this talent must be developed."- Mary Curie

Positive affirmations are a powerful tool for teaching your mind to think positively. Repeating them will help your mind build a positive attitude. Reading motivational and inspiring quotations every day can help you combat negative thoughts and cultivate optimism in yourself. Any negative incident should be approached with optimism, and you should strive to draw a good conclusion from it.

Keep in mind that your ideas influence your moods and behaviour. You should, therefore, instantly replace any negative thoughts that enter your head with positive ones. Even if things are bad, having an optimistic outlook will help you get through the challenging period without too much difficulty. Whatever the circumstances, make a commitment to be upbeat. Instead of worrying if things aren't going your way, keep working toward your objectives with an optimistic outlook, and you'll soon start to see wonderful results!

"Ability is what you're capable of doing. Motivation determines what you do. Attitude determines how well you do it."- Lou Holtz

CHAPTER FOUR

Your Determination Gives Unwavering Strength

"I am not judged by the number of times I fail, but by the number of times I succeed: and the number of times I succeed is in direct proportion to the number of times I fail and keep trying."
-Tom Hopkins

You'll never succeed if you don't strive for.

Everyone aspires to be successful, but the reality is that very few individuals do. However, if someone genuinely wants it, they can succeed, so it doesn't have to be that way. To do that, one must possess the necessary information and awareness of what it is that makes a person successful. And above all things, a person's thinking is what decides whether or not they will be successful. How to make sure you don't give up! If things don't go according to plan, you could occasionally feel like doing this; this chapter will teach you how to stop yourself!

I have gotten lots of results! I know several thousand things that won't work! " One of the most well-known figures in the history of invention, Thomas Alva Edison, is renowned for his many original concepts and works of art. He created revolutionary inventions, including the electric light bulb, the phonograph, batteries, and much more. He held over 1,000 patents, a record that was only recently broken. But despite his extraordinary achievements,

Edison frequently failed. In reality, it frequently took hundreds of attempts to get his experimentation just right.

When Edison was trying to come up with a new storage battery, it was precisely the situation. Walter S. Mallory, a close friend of Edison's, said that despite doing 9,000 trials, he had still not succeeded in coming up with a solution. "I am aware of thousands of things that are ineffective," Edition said to his friend Mallory.

"Our greatest weakness lies in giving up. The most certain way to succeed is always to try just one more time."-Thomas Alva Edison

Without a doubt, Thomas Alva Edison was one of the greatest inventors of all time. His 1,093 patents include the light bulb, the motion picture camera, and the phonograph, which is his most notable invention. He struggled a lot before finding success with his light bulb innovation, which demonstrates his strength of will. To find a filament for the light bulb, Thomas Alva Edison experimented with "two thousand" different materials. His aide cried out, "All our efforts are in vain," when none of them performed as expected. We have gained no knowledge. Oh, we have gone a long way and we have learnt a lot, Edison said with much assurance. We now understand that there are 2,000 components that we cannot employ to create a bright light bulb. Teachers at Thomas Edison's school claimed that he was "too ignorant to learn anything." His first two employments were terminated because he was "non-productive." Edison, a brilliant inventor, made a thousand fruitless efforts to create the light bulb. A reporter asked: How does it feel to fail 1,000 times? Edison answered, "I didn't err a thousand times." The light bulb was a 1,000-step creation. "

Accept the fact that every day and every second of your life will be filled with battle, and commit to waking up every day to fight that struggle so that any task you choose will reflect the hardship you have experienced.

“The 10,000-hour rule or the proverb "success is 1 percent inspiration, 99 percent perspiration" may be known to you.”

Sachin Tendulkar was born with the "eye of the tiger." It was my memory of Sachin Tendulkar's first international assignment, the 1989 tour to Pakistan. I can remember a pretty intriguing atmosphere from November 15, 1989, the day he made his test debuts. The 16-year-old with prodigious potential who was going to compete against people like Imran Khan, Wasim Akram, and Waqar Younis. Some others made fun of Sachin by using phrases like "Yeh khel payega ya nahi?" Also said, "Yeh toh baccha." Will this guy be able to play? He is young. However, Sachin was not a typical 16-year-old. He was a guy, extremely mature and committed to his game when he stepped onto the playing field. We were aware of his capabilities and his desire to succeed by exerting all of his effort. A few events that transpired throughout the trip stick out in my memory. They were trying to rescue a Test match in the fourth Test at Sialkot when Sachin joined Sidhu at 38 for four in the second innings. A Waqar Younis bouncer smacked Sachin square in the nose on a green track. Sachin was confused as he began to bleed heavily from a severe cut. It was surprising how quickly he snapped out of his trance and developed that expression in his eyes. You're familiar with the hit song "Eye of the Tiger." It was like that, and his eyes were burning with rage. He replied that he was oaky after splashing water on his face. Then Sachin came onto the pitch and scored four on the following ball! This 16-year-old was involved!

"The key to handling pressure situations like these is to keep yourself steady, follow your instincts and think clearly."
— Sachin Tendulkar

He has a strong enthusiasm for cricket. This particular event exemplifies his intense love of cricket. Sachin also played the whole 2003 World Cup with a wounded index finger. His finger was so seriously injured that he needed to travel to the USA for surgery after the competition. Tendulkar discusses how he overcame obstacles with the use of passion, preparation, and execution. When my goal came true, I was in the same locker room as Indian cricket's biggest names. "Being able to interact with them and train with them gave me the mental fortitude I needed to succeed on an international stage," said Tendulkar.

"If Destiny throws a stone at you, don't let it become a millstone. Make it into a milestone."

— Sachin Tendulkar

The magnificence of Sachin Tendulkar is beyond description. He is a true example to all athletes with his incredible determination, devotion, and enthusiasm for cricket. To imagine what he must have gone through over the course of these 24 arduous years in order to reach the great heights he has attained is mind-boggling. And to think he started his professional career abroad at the age of 16! Tendulkar, the only athlete from India to get the Bharat Ratna award, scored 34,357 runs in international competition in all three forms (18,426 in ODIs and 15,921 in Tests). He is the only batsman with 100 international hundreds in addition to this (51 Tests and 49 ODIs).

"A difficult time can be more readily endured if we retain the conviction that our existence holds a purpose – a cause to pursue, a person to love, a goal to achieve."

-John Maxwell

CHAPTER FIVE

Your Limitation Is Your Imagination

"If you always out limits on everything you do, physical or anything else, it will spread into your work, and into your life. There are no limits. There are only plateaus, and you must go beyond them." – Bruce Lee

Limitations only exist when you impose them on yourself mentally.

If you give your mind pleasant thoughts and guide it in the proper path, it has limitless power. It may be trained to do whatever you wish. Your thinking and viewpoint are greatly influenced by the narratives you tell yourself and the images you envision in your head.

"Limits like fears are often just an illusion." Michael Jordan

Your actions are influenced by your ideas, which in turn mould your reality. The limit is in your head, said Arnold Schwarzenegger. He had always believed that "as long as the mind can envisage the notion that you can achieve anything, you can do it, as long as you believe 100 percent." And the outcome of that belief is plainly seen to everyone. The limits are all made up and fictitious in your imagination. They get stronger the more you cave in to them. The more you give in to them, the more control they exert over you as they get stronger. Many individuals go through life living in mediocrity because they accept limiting ideas and neglect to access their inner strength. The majority of the time, mental obstacles are false self-imposed ideas about oneself that cause self-sabotage.

How to make sure you remain on path and finish what you started when the unexpected occurs! You will discover a highly useful approach in this chapter that is not present in any other chapter. There are a lot of suggestions to help you determine what you want in life in general! You won't ever run out of life-altering thoughts again. The most important step you must take to guarantee your success! Fortunately, this topic demonstrates how simple this is. Your systems determine how high you can fall. Here, you'll find a tried-and-true strategy that can help you succeed.

> "*A few injustices or tragedies may be more profound than denying someone the chance to strive or even hope because of a constraint that is imposed from without but is mistakenly believed to be from within.*"

The You-Factor offers the secret to living the life of greatness you were meant to live by weaving together personal experiences, useful ideas, and profound biblical truth. Everyone wants success in their lives. However, we all define prosperity slightly differently. Some people interpret it as having plenty of money and being wealthy. Others believe that happiness begins with perfect health or freedom. The Prosperity factor is your road map to achieving your goal and personal dream of success.

Nick Vujicic was born with phocamelia, a rare congenital disorder characterised by limb deformity. He has overcome the odds despite having very little foot by becoming a motivational speaker, getting married, and becoming a new father to Kiyoshi. Nick shares that he was fortunate to be born without limbs and legs, showing remarkable humility and sensitivity. For him, coping entails finding out how to live without something they have always known, which is a far more difficult task. How was this all made possible?

I watch in awe as Nick tells tales that highlight significant events in his life. He is very grateful for a small foot (or chicken drumstick, as he fondly refers to it), which allows him to do a lot of things, like wash his teeth, drive a car, use a computer, and more. With what he has, he has been able to lead a self-sufficient existence, produce four books, and inspire others. He says that comparing oneself to those who are better, richer, or more attractive all throughout one's life would only lead to unhappiness.

Gratitude has always been associated with leading a fulfilled life. Robert Emmons' study has shown that being appreciative has substantial psychological, social, and physical advantages. Gratitude practitioners frequently report stronger immune systems, greater sleep, and happier dispositions. Additionally, they report feeling more kind and less alone.

The goal of Nick Vujicic, an evangelist and international speaker of Australian descent, and his team at Life Without Limbs is to overcome boundaries, tear down walls, and create bridges that connect people. He has inspired millions of people across the world despite his disability. Nick is an excellent role model for practically everyone who has faced the toughest obstacles in life and yet wants to achieve their biggest dreams.

> "*When you tell yourself what you can or cannot achieve without first determining what you are actually capable of, you become your worst energy. These unfounded presumptions put a stop to your progress and keep you from achieving your goals and ambitions. Consequently, you are doomed to a life of mediocrity.*"

Jessica Cox, a pilot with no arms who learned to fly with her feet. Due to a rare birth abnormality, Jessica Cox was born without arms. She has continued to live her life to the fullest despite this. Ms. Cox has really accomplished and experienced more than most individuals do in a lifetime. She started her pilot training after earning her degree from the University of Arizona in 2005.

According to CNN, Cox, a motivational speaker who can play the piano, drive a vehicle, scuba dive, and even hold a third-degree black belt in karate, wants to inspire individuals with disabilities and has visited more than 20 countries. She frequently considers what her life would be like if she could turn back time and be born with arms. Not only would her life be drastically different, but she would also understand how powerful it is to live one's life in a way that has such a profound effect on others. She has had leaders and role models. And now that she has experienced it, it's her duty to provide the same for the next generation of arms. She told the CNN news channel. Despite her initial dread of flying, Cox quickly overcame it and concentrated on obtaining her licence. Cox told the media outlet, "I had multiple flying instructors and contributed to my training to find this out." Therefore, determining what would work through trial and error took three years.

Because many people place restrictions on their own potential. I hope these sayings motivate you to pursue your aspirations and live a life without boundaries. "Exceeding boundaries and establishing your own rules is sometimes the greatest way to learn." Stop putting yourself at a disadvantage. Recognize that the possibilities for what you can do with your life are endless.

What does it mean to "put boundaries in place"?

Why do we take them upon ourselves, exactly? When we create limits for ourselves, we determine that there are some things we are only capable of, certain distances we may travel, and certain things we only have a limited set of abilities. Why did we make this decision? Where did these concepts come from? Frequently, we create them without any tests or evidence. They stem from feelings of dread or failure, from messages we received as children, or from the fact that we have allowed the limitations of others to affect us. Your mind is what you feed yourself, just as your body is what you consume. All facets of your life are affected negatively by your thoughts.

"If you believe you are not capable of anything, your mind will provide you with all the evidence that you are not."

You'll start to see answers and breakthroughs if you change your perspective and convince yourself that you can do anything. Ignore the negativity within and around you and make the decision to only think of good ideas. Do that repeatedly, despite your feelings of helplessness, dejection, and lack of motivation. By giving yourself encouragement, you may direct your inner energy toward good expectations and look forward to the results of your work. It is essential to have a development attitude in order to push your boundaries.

It is essential to have a development attitude in order to push your boundaries. When you adopt a development mentality, you clearly communicate to your subconscious that nothing is out of your reach. You can learn anything you're enthusiastic about, develop your talents, and become whatever it is you want to be. There are no restrictions of any kind. Your mind starts to see the bridges instead of the streams, the solutions instead of the issues, and the road ahead instead of the hurdles with the appropriate sort of programming. The fundamental shift in how you view yourself that the growth mindset causes is what makes you unique and unlocks the doors to your future success. You must push past your limitations and leave your comfort zone in order to achieve your objectives and become the person you desire. Eleanor Roosevelt once stated, "You must do the things you believe you cannot do." You only become aware of your potential when you push past your limitations.

"Nothing can prevent you from succeeding and evolving into your greatest self if you train your mind and harness its immense potential.Have faith in your own potential, skills, and abilities. All of your hopes and dreams are attainable for you."

Things only seem challenging before you try something new or start working toward a goal. When you overcome mental obstacles, you feel at ease performing tasks and discover that they are simpler than you had believed. The human mind is hard-wired for simplicity and takes the easiest route to keep you safe from harm. It would always pick comfort over unfamiliarity, pleasure over pain, and leisure over hard work.

> "*The human mind is hard-wired for simplicity and takes the easiest route to keep you safe from harm. It would always pick comfort over unfamiliarity, pleasure over pain, and leisure over hard work.*"

As a result, you must flip the narrative and prepare your mind, teaching it to do what you desire. It's all in your head in the end, whether you succeed or fail, fight or give up, or live an ordinary or remarkable life. You must make the necessary effort. However, you must first let go of any mental restrictions and have confidence in your ability to bring your aspirations to reality. Your world is created by what you think and visualise in your head. When you have confidence in yourself, you'll start to attract opportunities, your skills will advance, and your chances of success will dramatically improve. You must understand that your inner world determines what you manifest in your outer environment. Since your inner world determines what you manifest in your outer environment, you must plant the seeds of positive thought if you want your efforts to have a positive result. Despite all of the opposition, justifications, and weak arguments, you must be proactive and take action. Just get going.Any worthwhile goal must be pursued with zeal.

"The only limit to your impact is your imagination and commitment." – Tony Robbins

CHAPTER SIX

Your Self-Belief Influences Your Success

"Every morning in Africa, a gazelle wakes up. It knows it must move faster than the lion or it will not survive. Every morning, a lion wakes up knowing it must move faster than the slowest gazelle or it will starve. It doesn't matter if you are the lion or the gazelle, when the sun comes up, you better be moving." -Roger Bannister

Self-belief and hard work will always earn you success.

The trip through life is not an easy one, and it gets even more difficult if you are working toward success in your endeavours. When things are difficult, your aspirations appear unattainable, and the circumstances are adverse, it is your conviction in yourself and your capacity to achieve your goals that keeps you going. When you have confidence in yourself, you work more diligently, passionately, and enthusiastically. You go into turbo mode because of the mental conditioning that says your efforts will pay off and you'll succeed; nothing can stop you from accomplishing your objectives. Your confidence will increase in direct proportion to how much you believe in yourself. You'll feel inspired to act, move beyond your comfort zone, seize new possibilities, take risks, and explore the unknown. Your confidence increases your self-assurance.

"Self-belief is what motivates you to take action and won't let you give up until you achieve your goals."

Self-belief is the first step toward success. You start on a good note and give yourself a head start when you have a strong sense of self-belief.Self-belief believes that you will succeed even before you start. You carry out all the actions of a champion because you behave and think like a successful person.As a result of your victory, your success has started to materialise.

Identity, significance, and perspective are the three dynamics that I name as being crucial to winning the war of the You-Factor. Knowing who you are and having a solid understanding of who you are establishes your identity. When you recognise your importance, you may realise the value and brilliance for which you were made. And if you grasp the concept of perspective, you may see your difficulties not as obstacles to success but as steppingstones to greatness. If you fully comprehend these three dynamics, you can control your You-Factor.

Healthy self-belief is neither arrogance, boasting, nor narcissism. Instead, it is a realistic yet upbeat assessment of who you are and what you are capable of. You are inspired to undertake things that you previously believed were impossible for you when you believe in yourself. You can take the first step, the next one, and then another step because of your faith. Before you know it, you're walking briskly along the road that once gave you anxiety.

"With each encounter, when we truly pause to confront fear, we acquire strength, bravery, and confidence." We need to take action on what we believe we cannot. " -Eleanor Roosevelt

When you have self-belief, no setback or failure can make you lose confidence or cast doubt on your abilities. You won't always succeed despite your best efforts; you'll make errors like everyone else and make blunders, miss opportunities, and perform poorly. But there is a distinction. Your confidence gives you power.

You have to do it, and Roger Bannister is an example of this. He achieved the unthinkable and broke the "Four minute" barrier because he was absolutely positive that he would succeed, not simply because he thought he could. Many thousands of attempts ended in failure. Both physicians and scientists concurred that it couldn't be done. Not only was it risky, but it was also impossible. "Anyone who tried to run a mile in under four minutes would perish in an idiotic endeavour." He had an incorrect bone structure, too much wind resistance, insufficient lung capacity, and a heart that could not withstand the effort.

"However ordinary each of us may seem, we are all in some way special, and can do things that are extraordinary, perhaps until then...even thought impossible."

— Sir Roger Bannister

Whatever angle you choose, they all agree that hard work is the secret to real success. People have been attempting to break the 4-minute barrier for years and years. Some came very, very close, but the record remained at 4:01.30 for about nine years as runners began to believe that perhaps, just perhaps, the experts were correct. Perhaps the human body had reached its limit, making it impossible. Then, on May 6, 1954, a chilly and rainy day in Oxford, England, a man by the name of Roger Bannister appeared to alter everything when, at the age of 25, he accomplished the unimaginable and ran the distance in 3:59.4. Everything that had previously been thought to be impossible became suddenly possible, and all preconceived notions that it couldn't be done were disproved.

In reality, he often imagined achieving the goal as part of his training to instil confidence in his mind and body. Before actually breaking the record, he had experienced what it was like to do so. Without seeing any tangible evidence that it was possible, he was the only one who could generate assurance inside himself.

Even more astounding than Bannister's inconceivable, world-record-breaking run is the fact that another runner achieved the same feat just 46 days later. And this time, he sprinted the distance in only 3.57.9 seconds, a whole 1.5 seconds quicker. Yes, another runner achieved the impossible not much longer than six weeks after Bannister.

However, as more and more athletes came to believe that it was feasible, more and more of them smashed the mark. By the end of 1957, almost three years after Bannister's unbelievable, record-breaking run, 16 athletes had also done the unthinkable and broken the four-minute barrier.How on earth is it even possible? How is it possible that other runners started to break the four-minute barrier so soon after Bannister did? Has human evolution had a rapid upswing? Did every runner suddenly start to improve? Did everyone alter their exercise and nutrition at the same time? Or was there another factor at play—something deeper?

You see, all it took was one man with a notion so deeply embedded in his head to challenge experts in his field and accomplish the seemingly impossible. You must act when you have such a strong belief in something and such a clear picture of it in your mind that it becomes your reality. Whatever it is, I don't care.

Roger Bannister is such a light and an example of mankind because of this. Not just because he was a fast runner or ran a mile in under four minutes, but also because he demonstrated to us that the only limitations we face are those that we place on ourselves. He accomplished the inconceivable, the unthinkable, and what both science and medical professionals believed could not be done.

"Believe in yourself! Have faith in your abilities! Without a humble but reasonable confidence in your own powers you cannot be successful or happy."

-Norman Vincent Peale

It doesn't matter if you start off with skill, knowledge, or competence. Self-belief is the first step toward success. You start on a good note and give yourself a head start when you have a strong sense of self-belief.

Self-belief believes that you will succeed even before you start. You carry out all the actions of a champion because you behave and think like a successful person. As a result, your success starts to materialise because success becomes a skill that feeds itself.

"Never let anyone tell you what you can or cannot do. Don't allow other people's limitations to restrict your vision. You will find a way if you don't give up on something you genuinely believe in."

You can do things you never imagined possible if you can get rid of your self-doubt and have faith in yourself. What is the relationship between accomplishment and self-belief? Self-belief is the foundation upon which you can build the life of your dreams. Your protection against the what-if scenario that occasionally enters your mind is self-belief. Self-belief keeps you going when you are aware that the deck is stacked against you, your opponent is stronger than you, and everyone believes that you can't compete with him.

The inner voice encourages you to follow your gut, rise to the occasion, and take measured risks. By doing so, you may expand your horizons and empower yourself to achieve greater things. High self-esteem and a feeling of self are characteristics of those who believe in themselves. They have unconditional love and acceptance for themselves and don't care what people think or say about them. Their own opinions are the only ones that matter to them.

All of your self-doubts, anxieties, and apprehensions are dispelled by self-belief. People with conviction are motivated from the inside out and exert great effort to achieve their objectives. Only when you have a strong belief from the inside out can you overcome obstacles and give every task you take on your best effort. When you decide to seek achievement, you will frequently face hardships and challenges. However, having confidence in yourself will give you the strength to act with unwavering dedication to your objective.

"No one is born with all the skills, abilities, or information; everyone learns in their areas of passion."

When you have confidence, you understand that you alone are accountable for your achievements and that, with enough willpower, you can accomplish everything you set your mind to. There is an abundance of information available, and there are no restrictions on the knowledge or skills you may pick up. The convenience of having everything at our fingertips in the digital era is a gift. All you need is an eagerness to learn and an open mind. When you have self-belief, no setback or failure can make you lose confidence or cast doubt on your abilities. You won't always succeed despite your best efforts; you'll make errors like everyone else and make blunders, miss opportunities, and perform poorly. But there is a distinction. Your confidence gives you power.

Neeraj Chopra created history when he won the men's javelin competition, becoming the first Indian to win an Olympic gold medal in athletics. Neeraj Chopra won India's first gold medal in the javelin throw at the 2020 Tokyo Olympics with a fantastic performance of 87.58 metres. But many years before this moment of brilliance, Neeraj Chopra, a chubby child who turned to sports to shed weight, faced intense pressure to slim down after blending his family of 17. At Tokyo's Olympic stadium, which should have been packed to the gills to witness his brilliance unfold, Chopra was nothing short of a rock star. Neeraj Chopra's metamorphosis from an overweight kid to the first Indian to win an athletics gold medal is a transformative but inspirational tale. He didn't even have to throw a personal best of 88.07 metres to get everyone to shout for him, as he always does. Only his second throw of the final round, the 87.58m one, was needed to win the gold. Along with winning the top spot in the 2017 Asian Championships, his other accomplishments include gold medals at the 2018 Commonwealth Games and the Asian Games. He is a 2018 Arjuna Award recipient as well. The tall, vivacious, and humble athlete's journey toward success began in 2011, when senior javelin thrower Jaiveer Choudhary of a neighbouring hamlet drew him into the sport.

You are aware of who you are and your abilities. You are inspired to follow your intuition and pursue your ambitions by your talent and faith. Rather than chasing after things that other people are striving for or what is trendy, you follow the objectives that connect with your inner self. Self-confidence gives you internal strength, so you may have high expectations for yourself and work assiduously to meet them. You don't feel pressured or driven to look for other people's endorsements or affirmations of what you accomplish. You are your own cheerleader and motivator.

Your thinking sets all of the boundaries. You have put yourself on the definite route to success the moment you decide to pick yourself up, depend on yourself, and have faith in your capacity to become an expert in your field. It doesn't matter if you start off with skill, knowledge, or competence.

" Your success would be defined by your own confidence and fortitudes"-Michelle Obama

Those who have read about Steve Jobs know that while he was still an outstanding leader, his success may not have always been attributed to his capacity for leading others. Everyone will tell you that networking and putting on a good show are key components of doing business, but Steve Jobs was able to think creatively and motivate others around him to work toward a shared objective.

Even if some of his contemporaries thought Steve was crazy, Apple wouldn't have developed the items that have now become standards if it weren't for his remarkable vision. The lesson of life? Steve Jobs kept coming up with fresh concepts, which gave him a competitive edge.

Steve Jobs is without a doubt the greatest commercial innovator in contemporary history, and for good reason. He was a technological pioneer and the creator of Apple, one of the greatest businesses in the world and a testament to Steve's unrivalled intelligence.

"Be a yardstick of quality. Some people aren't used to an environment where excellence is expected."- Steve Jobs

Steve Jobs was once expelled from his business and might have retired wealthy, but he persisted in creating and finally returned to Apple. Only because of his innovative and risky business strategies could he return to Apple. This lesson in life advises us never to give up seeking larger and better things. The life lessons Steve Jobs picked up along the road, such as how to persevere through adversity and discover passion in adversity, can be credited for his success. Even now, businesses still rely on his counsel since Steve's successes have become a how-to manual for aspiring business owners.

"Your time is limited, so don't waste it living someone else's life."- Steve Jobs

Steve Jobs was well known for being in quest of excellence constantly. His approach to product development was straightforward: only flawless items needed to be in the hands of consumers. Simply expressed, this kind of thinking may be used in all facets of business: don't sell something you wouldn't want for yourself.

In order to be as effective as you can be, it is crucial to be enthusiastic about the task you are doing. Steve lived this out every day. Never content with less than the best, he worked tirelessly to achieve excellence in all facets of his profession with the goal of building a company he could be proud of. To sum up, Steve Jobs was a role model and will be missed. He accomplished a great amount of work each day he lived on this planet, mostly as a result of his outstanding work ethic and desire to make the world a better place. He was, in our opinion, among the best motivational speakers of all time, and his modest teachings will endure for all time.

"People think focus means saying yes to the thing you've got to focus on. It means saying no to the hundred other good ideas that there are. You have to pick carefully."- Steve Jobs

When you enter an Apple Store, you will be welcomed at the door just like you would at a hotel. There is a concierge rather than a cashier at the Apple Store. Even a "bar" will be there, but instead of serving drinks, "geniuses" will be giving out advice. Jobs pushed everyone around him to think better, and that led to these inventions.

I visited an Apple store a few days ago and chatted with an expert who established the mobile phone retail business with his ground-breaking advice and insights . The first 150 Apple Stores were built by George Blankenship under the direct supervision of Steve Jobs. He was an expert at having great dreams, and he urged others to follow suit. Sometimes a question that makes individuals reevaluate their lives and their enterprises serves as the motivation.

"You can't just ask customers what they want and then try to give that to them. By the time you get it built, they'll want something new."- Steve Jobs

Whether you are aware of it or not, you engage in negotiations on a daily basis. A highly useful talent that isn't frequently taught is how to bargain without undervaluing yourself or deceiving the other side. Making a win-win outcome of a negotiation produces a positive image in the opposing party's mind, which enhances the likelihood of receiving more favours. Naturally, Jobs left college to follow his creativity. We are all aware of the outcome. His curiosity and intuition then, and throughout his life, allowed him to "stumble across" several sources of inspiration that would have a significant impact on his subsequent works.

Your self-belief factor reveals easy actions you can start using right away if you're ready for a significant change in your energy, perspective, and financial wellness. It delivers fresh tales, explains new processes, and offers new ideas. You always lean forward to the task at hand. No one can stop you from performing the work if you are motivated enough. Nobody can stop you from disclosing the truth. This will make it easier for all of you to confront the reality of life.

It takes a lot of confidence to maintain and accomplish your goals, and negative thinking about yourself is useless. It will just make you feel worse. Make the decision to maintain your good attitude; it will benefit you, especially through your most trying times. According to Will Smith, "You simply decide, and the universe is going to get out of your way." Will Smith went from being divorced and on the verge of bankruptcy to being a megastar.

Bill Gates reads more than 50 books annually, while Warren Buffett spends 80% of his day reading. Sam Walton picked the name

Wal-Mart over Walton-Mart to save money on signs, while Shark Tank's Kevin O'Leary would rather save $2.50 than spend it on a Starbucks. Although adopting the behaviours of these role models won't put you on the fast track to landing rockets on Mars, it can set you up for great success.

Following in the footsteps of others, especially successful ones, makes learning life lessons much simpler. And after viewing the biographical film "Jobs," which is based on the life of Apple co-founder Steve Jobs, I discovered that there are many lessons to be learned just from the way his persona is portrayed. Making goods that straddled the lines between art and technology, intuitiveness and design, was central to Jobs' ideology. He was able to live his philosophy and, in turn, inspire others because he was open to being inspired.

It's crucial to believe that people are fundamentally decent and intelligent and that, with the right tools, they can do great things. "Tools are simply that—tools." They either function properly or they don't. To put it another way, Jobs felt that the finest ideas come from the confluence of technology and the humanities. Thus, in order to succeed greatly and bring about revolutionary changes in the world, we must learn to prioritise this area.

"We're here to put a dent in the universe. Otherwise why else even be here?"- Steve Jobs

CHAPTER SEVEN

Your Disability Is Not A Liability

"You can't put a limit on anything. The more you dream, the farther you get."
-Michael Phelps

Believe in yourself; you are smarter than you believe you are.

You are inspired to undertake things that you previously believed were impossible for you when you believe in yourself. You can take the first step, the next one, and then another step because of your faith. Before you know it, you're walking briskly along the road that once gave you anxiety. With each encounter, when we truly pause to confront fear, we acquire strength, bravery, and confidence. We need to take action on what we believe we cannot.

Why do individuals seem to be stuck in a cycle of trying and failing to succeed? Why is it that even after we successfully lose weight, deliver a stellar presentation, or land that job, we frequently regain the weight or continue to feel incompetent? Why does it occasionally cause us to lose everything we have worked so hard to accomplish? Having the proper mindset and beliefs is the first step in achieving any objective, whether it be managing weight, overcoming poor self-esteem, or landing the dream job.

Sometimes humorous, occasionally eccentric, occasionally moving, and occasionally passionate. Here are some inspiring and thought-provoking stories about people with disabilities.

Everyone is aware of Michael Phelps‘ exceptional athleticism. Few people are aware that he suffers from Attention Deficit Hyperactivity Disorder (ADHD), and swimming is how he manages the excess energy his body produces. Many people think ADHD is a bad affliction, but Michael used it as motivation to swim. He recognised his primary weakness and channelled it into his greatest strength. You can take inspiration from him and use your flaws as motivation to strive harder or smarter. Michael Phelps is constantly in top physical shape to pull off his victories. He keeps up excellent levels of fitness and has a fantastic body. He puts a lot of effort into his exercises and attributes his general skill to strong genetics.

More than most people, Michael Phelps is aware that success does not come easily. The most decorated Olympian in history, while becoming a standout at a young age, put in the necessary effort over the duration of his career. He is aware of the impact of perseverance and hard effort as well as the places that these qualities might lead. Nothing else is getting in the way of our achieving our objectives and desires. Continue to be inspired, hungry, and driven. He is renowned across the entire world for becoming the most decorated Olympian in history. Olympic swimmer Michael Phelps is one of them. He has won 28 Olympic medals in total. There are 23 gold medals among them. The most incredible part is how he managed to accumulate all of these in only five Olympics. Michael is widely recognised for using the butterfly as his preferred swimming stroke. At the age of 31, he made the decision to stop competing in professional swimming after many Olympic victories. However, he won 5 gold medals and 1 silver medal, bidding the Olympic pools a happy farewell. He has a brave, tenacious, and resolute narrative.

Last but not least, the Phelps comment that is unquestionably the most well-known of all time and a favourite among fans. Given how frequently we have heard it (and read it) during our swimming careers, it may now feel like a cliche. But that is absolutely true. Michael Phelps points out that we are the only ones who have real limits.

When you are aware of the specific reason why your performance fell short of expectations, you get a particular feeling in the pit of your stomach. Give your best effort in order to avoid these emotions and all of the "what ifs" in order to do yourself a favour. Focus on the tasks you know you should do. Later on, you'll appreciate yourself. It's easy to occasionally go into a type of funk. It's simple to allow how your body feels to take control after a particularly challenging training session. You're feeling worn out and hurt, and you're unsure when the taper will start. But it's important to remember your initial motivations while you go through this unavoidable period. You set a goal for this season at the start of the year, whether you wrote it down or just had it in the back of your mind. It's not the right moment to stop pursuing it right now; instead, intensify your efforts.

One of the essential components of success is confidence. But even when we exert a lot of effort and self-control toward change, we can still trip and fall. How come this is the case? Even while we are mindful of what we desire, we can't help but think about the worst-case scenarios. Our imagination nearly always wins out when rationality and creativity clash! We can use our creativity to our advantage. However, if we have negative thinking despite our best efforts, it can also become a barrier to our achievement.

We genuinely communicate with ourselves through our ideas. Unfortunately, some people were not raised in loving, supportive, or stable families. They lacked that special someone to tell them they are intelligent, attractive, and deserving, or to compliment and inspire them as they achieved success. They might occasionally only come to attention when being naughty and not "performing" as they should.

When we were young, we lacked the critical faculties necessary to recognise hazardous notions. As a result, we took what was said at face value and subconsciously stored it. Once the subconscious mind is persuaded, it prompts the person to act on that belief. Now that we are older, we may rationally understand what attitudes and behaviours are healthy for us as well as what we need to do, yet change still appears to be so difficult to do. Change is resisted by our subconscious minds. Every change is viewed as a danger after a habit has been established. We could purchase self-help books, put out all of our cigarettes, or start yet another diet, promising ourselves that this time we would be even more disciplined.

Kavya Mukhija is a wheelchair user who was born with Arthrogryposis Multiplex Congenita. The young woman has overcome a number of psychological and physical obstacles to forge a joyful life for herself in which she accepts her impairment and shares a compelling message with the rest of the world.

> “*"I rely on my parents for everything, from taking a bath and getting dressed to obtaining a glass of water or lying in bed. Every evening, my mother drove me to physiotherapy to help improve my muscle strength. It irked me. Although my parents intended a simpler existence for me, I would cry in misery. They believed that my health would get better and that I would eventually be somewhat independent."*”

A work environment that is accessible to people with impairments helps them to work efficiently. But how frequently do ramps, tactile tiles, or Braille signage actually appear? This is a result of the low level of understanding of disability rights, inclusion, and accessibility. Additionally, people with disabilities have been surviving in a world that was not created for them. We don't even incorporate people with disabilities into our society because of a lack of awareness or just "forgetting" to create ramps or elevators. In fact, a lot of people still think that people who use wheelchairs should exclusively reside in medical facilities!

Even if it's not always simple to get back up after an accident or failure, some people manage it and inspire others. When a horrific catastrophe or heartbreaking situation occurs, most people lose hope. However, some people never give up and go on to inspire millions of others. Yes, I'm referring to Muniba Mazari, a person who is confined to a wheelchair yet nevertheless motivates others and advances society.

Muniba claimed that her time in the hospital was the hardest time of her life since she had to rely on people for even a sip of water. She occasionally felt thirsty in the middle of the night, but she was forced to go the entire time without drinking anything since she didn't want to wake the others up. After spending two years in bed, she was given permission to use a wheelchair.

How to be grateful after difficulties, after a serious vehicle accident that left Muniba Mazari unable to walk, she chose to live her life rather than weep. There are many inspiring people in the world, and each one has a unique life narrative. This is the tale of a lady whose wonderfully flawed existence has shaped who she is now. This is the tale of a woman who holds the opinion that sometimes our issues aren't so large, but we're just not big enough to deal with them. Let's examine Muniba Mazari's remarkable life story and how she came to be in this position. Muniba Mazari asserts that words have the ability to either make or ruin a person. They have the power to either restore your soul or irreparably harm it. Muniba Mazari has watched her life fall apart in front of her eyes since she was a small child, yet she has never given up. Many people have illnesses that render them permanently crippled, but the first thing they do is give up. One of them is this incredible angel who showed the world that everything is possible by rising from the ashes and standing higher. She served as an example for the rest of the globe, in addition to herself. Instead of running from her concerns, she faced them head-on and overcame them. In the end, we all come to the realisation that success, wealth, and celebrity are not the sources of true pleasure. It can be found in thankfulness.

Muniba exclaimed, "I was so thrilled when I sat in a wheelchair for the first time." What if I didn't have legs? "I now have two wheels," she declared. Her life then abruptly turned around. Doctors urged her to keep pursuing her goals and passion, which was painting. Muniba quickly made a reputation for herself in the art world and demonstrated that a wheelchair is no barrier to success. She is presently regarded as one of Pakistan's top painters and artists. She uses oil pastels as her medium, and her company is called Muniba's Canvas, with the tagline "Let your walls wear colours."

Muniba is now a recipient of several honours and often delivers inspirational talks at conferences all over the world. She is a representative of Pakistan on the coveted Forbes 30 under 30 list of the world's best young leaders, entrepreneurs, and game-changers. Her additional accomplishments include serving as the Body Shop's brand ambassador; being Pond's miracle mentor; being Tony & Guy's wheelchair model; and being one of the BBC's 100 Most Inspirational Women of 2015. Additionally, chosen as a U.N. goodwill ambassador in Pakistan, Muniba is promoting women's empowerment there. Many people find inspiration in her life story, and she also conducts several TED presentations.

People hide their disabilities so often. They attempt to hide it because they believe that being disabled is neither attractive nor seductive. However, it is not the case. You are not impaired just because you have a disability. It enlightens you. You get knowledge from it. You learn something from it that someone without it will never understand. Many people believe that a model girl who is six feet tall and weighs 100 pounds (1.8 metres, 45 kg) represents perfection. I have no idea what part of the world you reside in, but I seldom see girls like that on the streets. I do see individuals with impairments and differences, and I believe that is what we need to portray as being authentic and beautiful, despite what people may view as flaws.

> "*Everyone is entitled to the freedom to visit a restaurant. Everyone is entitled to the freedom to go on a date. Everyone is entitled to a chance and the right to employment. These goods, however, are not available to those with impairments.*"

Born in Australia on December 4, 1990, Dylan Martin Alcott, AO, is a former wheelchair basketball and tennis player as well as a radio personality and motivational speaker. Alcott competed for the men's national wheelchair basketball team of Australia, also referred to as the Australian "Rollers." He won the wheelchair basketball tournament at the 2008 Paralympics in Beijing at the age of 17, making him the youngest Rollers gold medal winner ever. He picked up wheelchair tennis again in 2014 in preparation for the 2016 Paralympics in Rio, where he took home gold in the Men's Quad Singles and Doubles. Because of his great performances in Rio, he was named the 2016 Australian Paralympian of the Year. Alcott received the Australian of the Year award and was elevated to the rank of officer of the Order of Australia in 2022.

"I don't get out of bed every day to play to win a tennis tournament, I honestly don't. I do it because I love it, but it also provides me with a platform to do what I really want: which is to continue to change the perceptions around disability."– Dylan Alcott

Arunima Sinha has received several honours for her courageous example. She was involved in a railway accident in 2011 and lost her left leg as a result of a fight with robbers. Arunima was unfazed by the conditions as she used her prosthetic leg to ascend Mount Everest.

"No matter how profound a loss, time always cures the agony, even though the scars remain," writes Arunima Sinha in her book Born Again on the Mountain: a narrative of losing everything and finding it again.

The first amputee from India to climb Mount Everest is Arunima Sinha. When she encountered a catastrophe on the train, it was reported by the media that she attempted suicide by jumping off the train. Later, her mother rectified the statement and clarified the situation with the media. Patients who have lost their legs often require 4 to 5 months to learn to walk again. Arunima Sinha, however, walked for two days. She did that because of her courage and drive. She raised the Indian flag for photos at the peak of

Mount Everest. When she was taking photographs, she had less oxygen available. When the opportunity to quit shooting pictures presented itself, she decided to do so anyhow, even if it meant risking her life. Due to a lack of oxygen, Arunima Sinha believed she would not make it to sea level. But it just so happened that she ran upon a British climber who had turned back in the middle of their ascent. He provided her with oxygen, which let her survive until she returned to the camp.

Arunima Sinha is a role model for young people, demonstrating her determination to pursue her dream of proving herself to the world. In 2015, the President gave her "The Padma Shri," the fourth-highest civilian honour. She also discussed the "Ted Talk" platform, which broadcast her success and motivated young people all over the world.

"By conquering all the seven summits I will prove that physical disability can never be a hindrance in achieving your life's goal if you have mental strength, strong willpower and firm determination."- Arunima Sinha

Our culture is exceedingly materialistic. It quickly forms a shallow opinion of a person based just on how they seem physically. Society does nothing to assist those in need; it doesn't accept those who are different in terms of how they appear, move, or even speak, and believes that they are superior to those who are disabled. But throughout history, several individuals have demonstrated that their physical limitations could not overcome their strong will, and in this article, we will learn about a few of those motivational figures.

"No matter how great a loss, time always heals the pain, even though the scars remain. Sometimes when you help someone else, you also end up helping yourself"

— Arunima Sinha, Born Again on the Mountain: a story of losing everything and finding it back

CHAPTER EIGHT

Your Failure Is Not Final

"If you fail, never give up because F.A.I.L. means 'First Attempt In Learning'. End is not the end; in fact E.N.D. means 'Effort Never Dies'. If you get No as an answer, remember N.O. means 'Next Opportunity'. So Let's be positive." — Dr. A.P.J. Abdul Kalam

Failure is a part of your process of excellence.

Since we are open systems, external inputs have an effect on us. The likelihood of encountering negative inputs is higher than the likelihood of encountering good ones, and bad inputs often have a bigger and more immediate influence on us than positive ones do. The goal of the book is to push you to become a semi-open system. Why does this matter? It indicates that you would feel much more productive and content if we could just take in the required negative stimuli while retaining the positive inputs. You won't have to deal with the emotional load of negative inputs that affect your day in an unfavourable way.

Even if it is difficult to accomplish, it is now more crucial than ever. Due to technology and social media, the amount of information we receive each day has doubled over the previous several years. This has dramatically raised the likelihood of encountering negative inputs. To ensure that nothing or no one interferes with your productivity and enjoyment, you must learn to filter out these negative inputs. You must get to a point where you can either avoid or at least lessen the harm caused by negative inputs. Being unbeatable means having the ability to sustain damage yet not lose.

"Excellence is a continuous process and not an accident."

What is an achievement? How does it appear? How can one accomplish that? I examine success in depth in this book. Life is setting you up for success, outlining what it is and isn't. To help you change your perspective and stop living a life of limitations, I will share the most inspiring stories of those who have faced defeat many times in their lives but have risen to make a difference on this planet.

"Many of life's failures are people who did not realize how close they were to success when they gave up." — Thomas Edison

Due to his inability to deliver language like a typical actor, people with speaking impairments are frequently passed over for roles in movies. But then came Rowan Atkinson, who, after facing several rejections, found success and cemented Mr. Bean's position in the audience's hearts with his own approach.

One of his well-known quotations is: "I adore strolling in the rain because no one can see me cry."

Rowan Atkinson maintained his enthusiasm and put in significant effort to achieve his goals. His goal was to get people to chuckle. He has achieved this via consistent work throughout the years. He started writing unique comedic routines after receiving multiple rejections. If you enjoy the Mr. Bean television series, you will probably enjoy Rowan Atkinson, who portrayed Mr. Bean. He is an English comedian, actor, and writer with a $150 million fortune. He is also regarded as a master of physical comedy and has played a variety of roles that showcase his comic abilities. But did you know the tale of his triumph?

He had a great deal of rejection and failure in his life, but he overcame those setbacks by using his vulnerability to become one of the most well-known comedians in the world. He was devoted to creating his own comedic routines since he loved to make others laugh so much. He subsequently realised that he could communicate clearly anytime he portrayed a persona other than himself. He used this as an inspiration for his acting, and this changed Rowan's life.

"I have to say that I've always believed perfectionism is more of a disease than a quality. I do try to go with the flow, but I can't let go. "- Rowan Atkinson

Even so, he tried out for various TV shows and auditions, but he was turned down everywhere. His acting development is hampered by his appearance, physique, and stammering issues. He demonstrated that you can be one of the most respected and adored performers even without a heroic figure and Hollywood face, despite his appearance and impairments that caused him to be rejected for many jobs.

Through one of his television shows, he showed us how to create our own pleasure without relying on anybody else. Rowan's confidence in himself helped him to overcome criticism, views, and prejudice. He didn't give up; instead, he persisted, and later on, life rewarded him.

"People assume that since I can make them laugh on stage, I can also make people laugh in person. That is not all the case. I'm really just a quiet, uninterested person who happens to act. Nowadays, we are seldom ever startled by what we see thanks to the media. "- Rowan Atkinson

One of the most well-known action figures of our time has severe dyslexia. Tom Cruise's condition never prevented him from performing actions that would cause a normal person to pass out in a couple of seconds.

"Nothing ends well; that's why it ends," he once stated.

He has the necessary amount of experience to support that claim, including his first-ever $1 billion box office success with Top Gun: Maverick. But what continues to amaze and excite audiences is Cruise's genuine enthusiasm for comedy. Tom Cruise rarely discusses his struggle with dyslexia in public or his chaotic household. One may suppose he was destined for success because he is a well-known actor across the world. As you'll see, though, that was just untrue. Tom Cruise and his three sisters were raised in a low-income family. He was often beaten by his controlling father, who ruled the family with an iron grip.

"I would go blank, feel anxious, nervous, bored, frustrated, dumb. I would get angry. My legs would actually hurt when I was studying. My head ached."- Tom Cruise

He gradually taught himself to study visually. To keep in character and recall his lines, he would focus on mental pictures. Tom Cruise overcame dyslexia through creativity, tenacity, and an optimistic approach. Above all, he chose a dream and made every effort to ensure that nothing would get in the way of it. He is currently one of Hollywood's highest-paid actors, with a net worth of $570 million. Anyone with dyslexia may find inspiration in Tom Cruise since he is a living example of how you can overcome your condition and achieve your goals.

"When I work, I work very hard. So I look forward to working with people who have that level of dedication. And I depend on that from everyone. "From the director to my crews that I work with" -Tom Cruise

The well-known Indian actress Kangana Ranaut was born in the Himachal Pradesh region's Mandi district. Kangana Ranaut's name comes to mind when we think about empowerment. She received several honours for her outstanding work in the Indian film industry, including 3 National Film Awards and 4 Filmfare Awards. She routinely appears on lists of the most fashionable and gorgeous celebrities in India. Additionally, she was included six times among Forbes India's Top 100 Celebrities. The fourth-highest civilian accolade bestowed upon her by the Indian government in 2020 was the Padma Shri. One of the trendiest and most divisive stars in India is Kangana. She is known for publicly voicing her thoughts, which usually causes issues. In addition to being lately in the headlines for all the wrong reasons.

"It speaks to the heart and the spirit and demonstrates how to live a life of artistic excellence."

All the motivation we could possibly need comes from Kangana's story of struggle in the profession, from being a nobody to winning three national awards for her performances in "Queen" (Best Actress), "Tanu Weds Manu Returns" (Best Actress), and "Fashion" (Best Supporting Actress). The extraordinary style of Kangana Ranaut, from small-town girl to actress Kangana Ranaut can handle the weight of the movie (and a dual character) on her own after nine years in Bollywood. She no longer needs a hero to support her.

Ladies and gentlemen, she has succeeded. Kangana Ranaut, formerly known as "the girl with curls," "Ms. Small Town," and "the actress that everyone disregarded," has established herself as a legitimate Bollywood star. Ranaut has demonstrated that she is a member of the exclusive group of performers who can ignite a passionate following that draws crowds to theatres. Even fewer women in Bollywood can make the same claim as the few males who can. But Ranaut does, and her latest triumphs have just added to the length of that list.

"The difference between average people and achieving people is their perception of and response to failure." — John C. Maxwell

Actor Nawazuddin Siddiqui made significant contributions to Bollywood and is renowned for his outstanding performances. He received his degree from the esteemed National School of Drama. His path had many highs and lows. In other words, it is both inspirational and emotional. Many aspiring Indian actors find inspiration in his life story.

Both maintaining a celebrity and becoming one are challenging tasks. Thus, it is not the issue. It is about having confidence in oneself. There are many people who will support you when you are playing your best, but there are fewer people who will do so when you are not.

"I would never be able to retain or sustain stardom."-Nawazuddin Siddiqui

When questioned about his numerous on-screen appearances, Nawazuddin Siddiqui responds that film is a fantastic medium for showcasing all of his personality. One individual is made up of a thousand different personalities, and he gets to experience each personality through the character he plays.

Our culture is more preoccupied with justice than the business world is. If you look at the newspaper marriage ads, it says that the girl or the guy should be fair, in addition to other things. The Indian market has a large consumer base for fairness creams. I want customers to understand that they are not required to become fair. I think it's important that those who advertise these goods shoulder some of the blame as well, since they might not be aware of how they're not just promoting their goods but also developing an inferiority mentality. That's not right!

In addition, if people believe I'm playing the victim card, the business will only recognise and value you for your job. With his unconventional parts and astounding performances, Nawazuddin Siddiqui demonstrates how a scientist turned actor can rock Bollywood to its very foundation. The ascent of Nawazuddin Siddiqui from poverty to wealth has served as an example for everybody. He has gone a long way from working odd jobs to support himself among the prominent performers in the industry.

"You may encounter many defeats, but you must not be defeated. In fact, it may be necessary to encounter the defeats, so you can know who you are, what you can rise from, how you can still come out of it." — Maya Angelou

Amitabh Bachchan, the biggest star of Bollywood, had several physical and financial hardships before he rose to fame as the millennium's biggest celebrity. These difficulties may tear someone to pieces. The rise of Amitabh Bachchan from obscurity to prominence in Bollywood serves as a terrific example for everyone who is battling obstacles and wants to do great things in life, not only those who wish to try their luck in the movie industry. Amitabh Bachchan, who is renowned for his tall stature and deep voice, has been rejected several times as a result of these two attributes. Because tall performers were not commonly used at the time in movies, he was turned down by producers, and he was also turned down by All India Radio because of his heavy voice when he auditioned for a radio jockey. Amitabh has experienced a number of failures during his life. But he accepted them and used them to pave the way for his achievements.

"Change is the nature of life, but challenge is the aim of life. So always challenge the changes not change the challenges" – Amitabh Bachchan

He made his Bollywood debut with the film Saat Hindustani, for which he later won a national award. Following the success of this film, he battled for two years to land a part in Anand and Zanjeer, which radically transformed his life. Nobody promised that life would be simple. Big B was slowly moving up the ladders of success when he had an accident on the Coolie set, which caused everyone to fear that Amitabh Bachchan would not survive. But he is a natural survivor since he bounced back fast and resumed his acting career. Unfortunately, the accident caused him to contract an illness that causes depression and weakness, and he is still battling it. Since then, he has developed into the Shahenshah of Bollywood and is one of India's wealthiest actors. After that, he received a call to host "Kaun Banega Crorepati," but his wife Jaya Bachchan objected, saying it wouldn't be appropriate for a famous actor like Amitabh Bachchan to anchor a TV show. Beggars can't be choosers, Amitabh Bachchan said in response. According to a statement made by Amitabh Bachchan, "Bad luck may either ruin you or expose the person you are."

He was able to rise above all the rejections and succeed greatly because of his perseverance and devotion to his objective. He acknowledged his shortcomings, which enabled him to keep becoming better. In one of his interviews, he advised everyone that "accepting and learning from your errors can help you become a better person." The life of Amitabh Bachchan teaches us that in order to attain great success, we should never linger on the past. Instead, we should always learn from it.

"If you're trying to achieve, there will be roadblocks. I've had them; everybody has had them. But obstacles don't have to stop you. If you run into a wall, don't turn around and give up. Figure out how to climb it, go through it, or work around it."

The mere mention of Amitabh Bachchan is enough to send chills down your spine and inspire deep admiration in your heart. This living great has delivered not just outstanding performances but also undeniably unmatched depictions throughout the course of a career spanning more than four decades. He is one of those performers who immerses himself so fully in the role that viewers frequently lose sight of the fact that they are watching a movie. He was able to rise above all the rejections and succeed greatly because of his perseverance and devotion to his objective. He acknowledged his shortcomings, which enabled him to keep becoming better. Taking motivation to advance in life from none other than Amitabh Bachchan, who is regarded as a household synonym for the term "role model."

"Don't fear for facing failure in the first attempt, because even the successful Maths starts with 'Zero' only."

— Dr. A.P.J. Abdul Kalam

CHAPTER NINE

Your Hard Work Is Crucial To Your Success

"If four things are followed - having a great aim, acquiring knowledge, hard work, and perseverance - then anything can be achieved."-A. P. J. Abdul Kalam

A determination to succeed ensures success.

How often have you heard that success comes from hard work? Undoubtedly a great deal, and it's true! Success is mostly dependent on effort, and this is true for many different reasons. Let's first discuss why working hard matters before we go into our arguments for why it's essential for success. Working hard enables you to gradually improve your level of self-discipline. Even though procrastination may make even the simplest chores more difficult to complete, we occasionally nevertheless self-destruct. Sometimes we don't even know why we do it! But if you are committed to working hard, self-control will come. This is another another example of why perseverance is essential for success.

"Working towards your goals and dreams can be challenging because the path to success is always a bumpy one."

Because people like to reward those who are willing to put up the effort necessary to complete all duties in order to succeed in life, hard work is something that has to be recognised. A person with discipline, devotion, and resolve to succeed in life is someone who works hard enough. You can achieve anything with effort. We have heard this piece of advice so frequently that its original meaning has been obscured. The issue is that despite our seeming laborious efforts, nothing seems to be happening. Many worthwhile goals in life need a lot of hard work to be accomplished. It's possible that working hard isn't always enjoyable or desirable. When you put off a difficult job, issues may develop in a variety of ways later. Laziness, which has a variety of negative effects on our lives, can be encouraged by avoiding hard labour.

In today's world, successful individuals are easy to come by. Every time we turn on the television, we see pictures of sportsmen being celebrated for their victories. We read articles in newspapers and publications about successful businesspeople scheming for their next lucrative investment idea. Our favourite actors and actresses may be found in movies as well, and they frequently amass more wealth through their labour in a single year than some of us will ever see. The media is prepared to show us the outcomes of these people, but they omit to reveal the processes involved. All of these folks put forth a lot of effort and commitment to get where they are. People compete for top honours and grades in school and college, for better positions at work, and to launch their own businesses in our world of continual competition. I will share the most inspiring stories of those who used their indomitable perseverence to accomplish their goals on this planet.

"I've missed more than 9,000 shots in my career. I've lost almost 300 games. 26 times, I've been trusted to take the game winning shot and missed. I've failed over and over and over again in my life. And that is why I succeed."- Michael Jordan

Any NBA fan, or anybody for that matter, will immediately mention one player when asked who the greatest basketball player of all time is. Basketball legend Michael Jordan is regarded by the association, the public, and even his fellow players. Michael, according to those who saw him grow up, was competitive in practically everything. He was a competitive person who actually hated losing. He thus took his exclusion from his high school's varsity squad quite personally. Most people agree that Michael Jordan is the best basketball player to ever play the game. He won four gold medals with USA Basketball, including two at the Olympics, and was twice recognised as the sport's top male athlete. He served as the NBA's spokesperson for more than ten years. He decided to change careers after that. How could a guy walk away from success when he was at the height of his power?

"My attitude is that if you push me towards something that you think is a weakness, then I will turn that perceived weakness into a strength."

- Michael Jordan

You had best start looking for its underlying causes if you want to cultivate success. Successful people understand that failure is the most beneficial experience in life. Our errors ultimately guide us in the correct direction. Early in his career, Michael Jordan made the decision to accept failure, learn from it, and do his best the next time.

> "*If we don't attempt it, we might never find out the outcome. No matter how many excuses we give ourselves why something won't work, if we don't attempt it, nothing will ever change.*"

There will always be challenges in our path to achieving our objectives. They shouldn't, however, prevent you from making the initial move. Obstacles are there to be overcome. The fact is that if you do nothing, nothing will ever change, and there is no other option except to try. Behavior is contagious. You'll succeed if you take the initiative and are consistent in your efforts. He was the first to understand that fear was a myth, which allowed him to work more and dream greater. The biggest barrier to success is the fear of failing.

> "*Humans are so afraid of failing that it prevents us from taking any action, yet the irony of life is that if we do nothing, we are destined to fail. Isn't that contradictory?*"

It's crucial to understand that the only limitations are those we impose on ourselves; in this case, the limitation is the delusion of fear. But you don't have to let challenges stop you. Do not turn around and give up if you hit a wall. Find a way to scale it, get through it, or go around it. Michael Avoid wasting your time and energy by worrying when you encounter a bottleneck. One solution exists — take a moment to collect yourself. Use this as motivation to be tough rather than allowing the pressure of the moment to bring you down. Remind yourself of why you must succeed and use that motivation to follow your ambition, which is what truly counts. The game has its ups and downs, but you must never lose sight of your own objectives, and you must never allow yourself to lose out of indifference. Failures, the opinions of others, his personal issues, team members, what the media said about him, celebrity, and many other issues had to be dealt with by him. But he never stopped concentrating on his goals. He never let anything from the outer world enter his head or heart. He maintained his vision and remained faithful to what he believed in.

A person with discipline, devotion, and resolve to succeed in life is someone who works hard enough. We've all heard the sayings, "There is no quick fix to success" and "Nothing worth having comes easily," but how many of us have actually lived by them? Sometimes in life, our goals and ambitions appear insurmountable, and we begin to lose patience. As a result, we start looking for shortcuts since we are exhausted and believe that our efforts are going in vain. Although the road to hard work is not always easy, the end result will be worth all the challenges, so trust me when I say that it will eventually pay off. Everyone must demonstrate a dedication to consistent hard work that will take them to the pinnacle of accomplishment if they are to accomplish anything in life.

> *"Hard labour cannot be substituted for Take a look at these inspiring sayings about hard work from some of history's greatest performers if you or your team are feeling worn out, overworked, or just "not in the mood" to work. You'll undoubtedly become inspired and get back on the road to success!"*

India's most outstanding female batswoman, Mithali Raj, has accomplished a lot in her two-decade international career. She bowls right-arm leg breaks and bats right-handed in the opening position. The only female cricketer to cross the 7,000 run threshold in Women's One-Day International matches, Mithali is the leading run-scorer in women's international cricket. Mithali Raj became the top run-scorer in women's international cricket in July 2021 during the third women's One-Day International match against England. She surpassed the previous mark of 10,273 runs set by Charlotte Edwards.

"I hope my journey inspires young girls to pursue their dreams."
-Mithali Raj

To become famous and successful, one must put in a lot of effort. Raj travelled to the India Women's Cricket Team's One-Day Internationals and Test matches. Because of the enormous skill pool, she was also rumoured to have played in the 1997 Women's Cricket World Cup at the young age of 14. Age wasn't included in the final selection, though.

Nevertheless, two years after she was left off the final list, Mithali Raj made her one-day international debut. Her 114 runs, which were too unbeatable, were what made her debut the most remarkable and unforgettable. The first test, played in 2001–2002 against South Africa, came shortly after. Since that time, nobody has turned back. On August 17, Mithali Raj successfully surpassed the record for the highest run in a women's test during the same season. She received numerous honours, including the Arjuna

Award in 2003, the Padam Shri Award in 2015, the Wisden Indian Cricket Player of the Year Award in 2015, the Youth Sports Icon Excellence Award at the Radiance Wellness Conclave in Chennai in 2017, the Vogue Sportsperson of the Year Award at Vogue's 10th Anniversary in 2017, the BBC 100 Women List in 2017 and, more recently, the first Indian woman cricketer to be conferred with the prestigious Major Dhyan Chand Khel Ratna Award in 2022.

> "*We must develop a love for the pursuit of goals and the sacrifices required in order to differentiate ourselves from the competition. Success comes to those who are willing to travel the difficult road and work toward difficult goals.*"

Without the so-called "work smart," I don't believe in luck or hard effort. It's not only about working hard; it's also about managing your time, resources, and thinking to get greater results."When it comes to things like team selection or job promotion, we will end up blending in with the herd if we choose the basic and straightforward routes in life.

There is no quick route to success; only steadfast labour may make one's life's goals and aspirations a reality. We frequently hear people's justifications for giving up. "It wasn't meant to be," "It wasn't enjoyable anymore," or "Life is all about having fun" are typical lines of speech that are used in response. It's important to note that our minds are capable of creating whatever mental state we give them. Instead, we should impose a commitment state that will enable everyone to realise their own goals.

> "*A person who has expertise in a certain sector is more likely than others who lack experience to accomplish their life's goals and can operate shrewdly and effortlessly.*"

This is still, without a doubt, the most difficult part of achieving successful objectives. What drives some people to relentlessly pursue their dreams while other people give up when things become tough? We get experience via hard labour, which enables us to learn a lot of new things. We may use this experience to develop clever thinking skills to successfully address a challenging issue. A person's ability to solve problems is enhanced through experience.

> *"Man needs his difficulties because they are necessary to enjoy success. Climbing to the top demands strength, whether it is to the top of Mount Everest or to the top of your career. Great dreams of great dreamers are always transcended."*

A million people can smile because of MS Dhoni. He has been doing it since the early 2000s, when he first became one of Indian cricket's most recognisable figures. Dhoni has become one of the most admired cricket players in the world thanks to several notable on-field accomplishments. The captain of the Chennai Super Kings, who has left the international stage, never ceases to win over his admirers. Dhoni is adored by the public for more reasons than just the fact that he is the most successful captain India has ever produced. However, due to his attitude on the job, as a result, he is known as "Captain Cool."

I occasionally ponder how someone can maintain their composure in the face of so much pressure and expectation. You must be honest with yourself and with others. In life, you must be realistic and willing to take chances. However, you also need to be pragmatic. We all want to replicate Dhoni's calm demeanour, which has made him popular. Even in the most challenging games, we could always count on him to smile. His cool demeanour earned him the position of team captain. He had become his captain, in addition to realising his goal of playing with his hero Sachin. He helped the side to a resounding win in the ICC T-20 World Cup in 2007. He never stops inspiring the next generation with his outstanding leadership and original thoughts. Bollywood paid its respect to his brilliance with the film "Dhoni: The Untold Story." There are a lot of Inspirational qualities of MS Dhoni which makes him an idol for many youths.

"I believe in giving 100%on the field and I don't really worry about the result if there's a great commitment on the field. That's a victory for me."

-MS Dhoni

MSD had seen a dream that many people dreaded seeing. Dhoni, who is from the little village of Ranchi, dared to dream and used bravery and guts to make that goal come true. From an early age, he looked up to cricket legend Sachin Tendulkar and Bollywood star Amitabh Bachchan. He began his work with the Indian Railways as a ticket collector. He ultimately made it to international cricket in 2003 because of his dedication and never-say-die attitude. Dhoni, though, had a loftier aspiration, one that made him the greatest cricket skipper to represent India.

"*Aim for the stars, and you might just hit the moon, as the saying goes.*"

Dhoni was known as an aggressive batter from a young age, but he didn't allow his ego to get in the way of picking up tips from other players. He picked up the helicopter shot from his pal, which eventually turned into one of Captain Cool's signature poses. In his school, Dhoni was the talk of the cricket team, and everyone used to admire him. Everyone around him was sad when he was rejected from the U-19 squad, but Dhoni made the decision to have a celebration. He put forth more effort to achieve where he is now because he valued the reality check provided by the snub. Dhoni used to finish his three-hour exam in only two and a half hours so he could head out and practise with his club. He balanced his love with his academics. He continued to attend practises even after starting a full-time job and working long hours every day at the train station. Dhoni held a regular government position. His family was content, and he might have led a prosperous life as well. Instead, he made a huge leap.

> *"The sensation of zeal you have from someone or something that provides you with fresh, imaginative things to accomplish is referred to as inspiration."*

When we are young, we create goals and aspirations that we want to achieve. In order to do that, we need to have the necessary information, abilities, and, most importantly, confidence to make all of these things stronger. For the same reason, we make an effort to follow anybody who can provide us with the support we need to accomplish all or any of these things, as doing so motivates us to pursue our aspirations. You get self-assurance that you can achieve something when you see that person or hear their remarks. Our parents are the first people who inspire us all because they help us develop the confidence we need to begin thinking rationally.

Over the past five years, this has been my area of interest. After observing human behaviour, I came to the conclusion that success is only possible for successful people because they have an insatiable appetite for achievement. When you have a burning desire to succeed, obstacles and setbacks become nothing more than speed bumps.

> *"Roadblocks and failures become speed bumps in your way when you have an unquenchable appetite combined with dedication and effort to accomplish a goal."*

You will get various experiences via hard labour, which will strengthen and improve you as a person. Simply be patient and believe in yourself. We want to be respected by those around us and have our thoughts valued. This is exactly what hard work and self-esteem boosting bring us. People always value those that put in the effort and are aware of their potential, regardless of how successful they are currently or will be. Working hard will help you improve every day and every moment. We frequently reflect on our past and ask ourselves, "What have we learned?" Working hard makes us better in every way; it turns a novice into an expert. Growth is not possible without effort.

"You can't connect the dots looking forward; you can only connect them looking backwards." So you have to trust that the dots will somehow connect in your future. You have to trust in something—your gut, destiny, life, karma, whatever. This approach has never let me down, and it has made all the difference in my life. " -Steve Jobs

According to a report, four out of ten people are leading unhappy lives. In all honesty, we have no idea what will occur tomorrow or a year from now. Many people have been heard expressing, "I wish I had done it before." due to the passage of time. They only wish they had put in more effort when it was necessary. You can live a life without regrets if you work hard. You won't ever have to regret not doing something since it will provide you with the foundation for a brighter future. Images, ideas, and literature are what people in the twenty-first century need to continually push themselves in a positive direction. While doing this, we fail to remember that drive and optimism result from effort. With hard effort and the sensation it brings, you'll be able to maintain your optimism for a longer time with hard effort and the sensation it brings. All of us have fallen head over heels for someone, whether it be a person with a lovely personality, someone we admire, or someone we aspire to be. We must, therefore, give our lives significance while we are living them. Without putting up effort and striving, nothing is possible.

> *"In order to realise your dream, you must first take the first step in that direction. You must give your all, regardless of where you are in the process of creating yourself or if you already have a life purpose."*

Having a single objective is the best way to make the most of your life. Having a goal is crucial, regardless of how large or small it is. And when you set a goal like that and work hard and dedicate yourself to it every day, you can achieve it and become the person you were meant to be. At this point, I believe that you have an understanding of how hard work and perseverance enable you to maximise your potential and turn your efforts into both monetary and non-monetary advantages that steadily grow over time.

"The three ordinary things that we often don't pay enough attention to, but which I believe are the drivers of all success, are hard work, perseverance, and basic honesty." -Azim Premji

CHAPTER TEN

Your Willpower Outweigh All Challenges

"Your work is going to fill a large part of your life, and the only way to be truly satisfied is to do what you believe is great work. And the only way to do great work is to love what you do. If you haven't found it yet, keep looking. Don't settle. As with all matters of the heart, you'll know when you find it."- Steve Jobs

Similar to a muscle, willpower requires continual nurturing.

You can't just admit that you made a dangerous choice at some point. To achieve what you want, you must be prepared for the sort of ability that is actually required. You must, nevertheless, take chances in order to succeed in life. Being honest in life is crucial to you.

> "*Every challenge you encounter has a single underlying question: how do you deal with yourself? An inability to manage what I refer to as the "You-Factor" is at the root of all of your stumbles, errors, and failures. &; The You-Factor is about managing yourself and your entire life properly, more so than self-worth or self-respect, even beyond character and sense of purpose.*"

No matter what your career, you must take challenges and come out of your comfort zone, and your humble background can't be an excuse if you fail. It is quite challenging to succeed in life if you don't respect others, whether they are your own or anybody else's. Let's imagine that when you enter any large building, you must treat everyone equally, from the first man you encounter to the managing director, for example. Go through the challenging time; struggle through it, but if you can do it with a grin, I am giving those great examples of people, perhaps five people, who set examples through their lives and can truly pull it off. Because we sometimes complain about life and the difficult times, it's vital to remember that it's going through the difficult moments that will really help you become a better person. I hope it is the start of something amazing and mind-blowing for you. This chapter illustrates how your thoughts may impact your mental, emotional, social, and physical health. It also covers the subject of how your willpower and visions might help you achieve inner tranquilly. A step-by-step examination of overcoming the internal obstacles to achievement may be found in from passion to peace.

> "*You must restrict or eradicate unproductive behaviours while imposing new habits that boost productivity if you want to have the desire and motivation required to consistently put out the level of effort required for productivity.*"

Oprah Winfrey's inspiring but painful success story Oprah had a difficult upbringing, growing up in poverty as the child of a single, underage mother. Because of the sexual assault she endured as a youngster, she had a difficult, rebellious adolescence. When she was thirteen, she fled her home. Oprah, despite having a challenging background, refused to let the past dictate her future. She served as proof that no matter what challenges we encounter, with passion, perseverance, and hard work, we can do anything. She had a variety of odd occupations as a child before getting a job as the local news anchor at a tiny radio network. She later began her own chat show while working for a TV station. She became a fan favourite thanks to her moving performance in that programme. Her television programme thus became one of the most popular programmes ever.

"Passion is energy. Feel the power that comes from focusing on what excites you" – Oprah Winfrey

Oprah had a lot of hardship as a child as a result of poverty. So, as she rose to fame, she gave money to the poor in an effort to make the world a better place to live. She is regarded as one of the greatest philanthropists of colour and one of the most powerful people in the world today. She has a US $3 billion net worth, placing her among the all-time most prosperous businesswomen. Oprah has been dubbed the most influential woman of her generation by Life magazine. According to Business Week, she is the biggest African American philanthropist in American history.

"Often we don't even realise who we're meant to be because we're so busy trying to live out someone else's ideas. But other people and their opinions hold no power in defining our destiny."- Oprah Winfrey

The Virgin Group is owned by English business magnate and philanthropist Richard Branson. The Virgin Group, which began with Virgin Records, currently includes more than 400 businesses. Branson, a serial entrepreneur, has had a remarkable life characterised by ups and downs. With his unwavering attitude, he has converted his setbacks into steppingstones for achievement. He has accepted his times of triumph and adversity. Branson's story will demonstrate that consistent labour, learning from mistakes, self-discovery, and tenacity lead to enormous success and progress for individuals and society whenever Virgin Galactic wants to launch non-astronauts into space. His way of thinking also shows how mistakes in the past just serve as more inspiration to go on and achieve new objectives. Richard Branson is unquestionably one of the world's most flamboyant and prosperous businessmen. Take advice from his stirring remarks.

"My interest in life comes from setting myself huge, apparently unachievable challenges and trying to rise above them."- Richard Branson

Three qualities are important to Sir Richard Branson when evaluating corporate success: leadership, connections, and enjoyment. Profits come when everything else is in place, and Branson certainly understands how to make things fall into place based on his tremendous financial profile. Richard Branson, a multibillionaire, has said that he finds it difficult to keep track of all the companies he owns. His net worth exceeds US $5 billion, and the British government knighted him for his contributions to business. He has a well-deserved reputation for success.

"You don't learn to walk by following rules. You learn by doing, and by falling over." -Richard Branson

Branson founded Virgin Atlantic Airlines in 1984 to improve the flying experience for customers. His new business almost collapsed before it even got off the ground because he recognised a huge opportunity but lacked experience. A swarm of birds crashed into an engine during the first test flight of Virgin Atlantic's lone aircraft, a chartered Boeing 747, resulting in significant damage. Without a functioning plane, the airline was unable to obtain certification to begin transporting passengers, and it was also unable to secure funding for repairs. Branson maintained his optimism rather than succumbing to fear or quitting. He reorganised his businesses rapidly and borrowed funds from other projects to complete the repairs. His company received the necessary clearance, and Virgin's first flight from Gatwick to Newark was a success.

Branson is a real adventurer who pushes his boundaries in both business and life. We can all take a cue from his bravery. Every entrepreneur, from those just starting in their garages to the highest C-Suite executives, may benefit from his encouraging comments from economic interviews, social media postings, and leadership books.

"We deify willpower and self-control - and mock its absence. People who achieve through remarkable willpower are 'strong' and 'heroic.' People who need help or structure are 'weak.' This is crazy - because few of us can accurately gauge or predict our willpower."-Marshall Goldsmith

You might not be aware of it (yet), but God wants to use your prosperity to win over the unconverted. There are occasions when success does come with some kind of quantifiability in the perspective of the outside world. However, even if your success doesn't come with a lot of money or other tangible belongings, people will still be drawn to you because of the way you live your life.

The well-known British novelist, who has a tenacious mind and a generous heart, is unquestionably the deserved recipient of all the accolades received worldwide. She carved her way into the reader's heart with the first book in the Harry Potter series and has been living there ever since, pledging never to leave. She emotionally collapsed as a result of her terrible marriage, experiencing domestic abuse, and falling into a deep despair. She was on the edge of being classified as "poverty-stricken" since she was a single mother working in a coffee shop for a small wage.

"It is impossible to live without failing at something unless you live so cautiously that you might as well not have lived at all, in which case you have failed by default." — J.K. Rowling

However, neither she nor true heroes wear capes. A positive outlook has a significant role in how fate plays out. Her writing was the only thing that kept her company during this protracted period of hopelessness and sadness. something she clung to tightly. By writing on paper napkins while working as a server, she demonstrated her desire to unwaveringly trust in her ideas and the likelihood that they will be wonderfully realized. Rowling always anticipated becoming a writer. Her website states that she knew she wanted to be a writer as soon as she learned what they were. But it didn't only take wishful thinking. While on a delayed train from Manchester to London, she began writing the Harry Potter books.

As Rowling imagined each character, the plot began to take shape. She jotted down the names and magical abilities of every single character and spent the following five years scripting the stories for each book. The stories are so fantastic because of this meticulous attention to detail.

The "J.K. Rowling" story was one of many that I got the chance to read. The abrupt loss of her mother left her in shock when she first had the inspiration to write Harry Potter. And at that point, she had to stop working on the book of her dreams. She was totally upset by her mother's unexpected death and was unable to continue working. Why do we presume that women are weak and unable to manage their lives on their own if they like their exits? After reading several successful accounts of women who had to battle on their own without any support, I found the assertion to be utterly incorrect.

> *"The key to realizing a dream is to focus not on success but on significance -- and then even the small steps and little victories along your path will take on greater meaning."*

Don't just relax. Take the initiative to make your aspirations a reality. You'll soon feel inspired and perceive new possibilities. You will be able to overcome obstacles and cultivate your own abilities. Learn how to calculate "Estimation of Effort" to make sure you surpass your goals. Learn about the fallacy of time management. Discover the precise causes of failure and success. You own the precise formula for problem-solving. By definition, extreme success is outside the bounds of customary behaviour. Take Tremendous action with your efforts , remove luck , and lock in massive success rather than acting like everyone else and accepting ordinary outcomes.

> *"I have no secrets, just my dedication and my passion: Cristiano Ronaldo insists there are no secrets to his success"*

Do you know Dwayne "The Rock" Johnson's origins? You undoubtedly already know how accomplished an actor he is. It's reasonable to say that he has a unique origin story that deserves to be the subject of a film or television series all on its own. Let's examine the "rags to riches" story of Johnson's rise to fame in more detail. For him, success might have appeared inevitable, but it wasn't. He tried his hand in the Canadian Football League before getting cut after sustaining injuries in college. He discovered that he was out of money and football. It wasn't until Johnson took on a very different persona that people began to take notice of him. In what is known as a "heel turn," he changed from being a hero to a villain, or in wrestling terms, from being a babyface to a heel, in what is known as a "heel turn," and after that, he was simply referred to as "The Rock."

"What's the key to success? The key is that there is no key. Be humble, hungry, and the hardest worker in any room. With drive and a bit of talent, you can move mountains. "- Dwayne Johnson

His persona changed into one who was haughty, used a lot of catchphrases, and spoke in third person. Johnson continued to sporadically appear for WWE, but by the early 2000s, his career as a professional wrestler was all but over. He thereafter started appearing in several Hollywood films. He first began with straightforward yet lucrative action movies like The Rundown and a Walking Tall remake. He then moved on to projects with higher budgets. Because we are basic beings, we always fall in love with compelling narratives. Every person that lives on Earth has a story to tell, and those stories might be upsetting, terrible, happy, or a combination of all those feelings.

Everyone loves tales of rags to riches. People enjoy hearing tales of valiant guys who battle against all difficulties to become among the richest people in the world. We are never tired of being amazed by butterflies. Everything and anything makes it genuinely majestic, including its enduring beauty and its mobile wings. But is that really the cause of our affection for butterflies? Is it only because it is beautiful? Never. The stories of butterflies—their struggle, their attempt to hide from the world, their quest for freedom, and their triumph—are what captivate us.

The last category is the one that consistently triggers our "inspirational nerves." A butterfly's life tale and Dwayne "The Rock" Johnson's life story both fit into this category. The man we see on tabloid and magazine covers now only spreads the wings of success and welcomes the sun, but he too had hardship in the past.

"The wall! Your success is on the other side. You can't jump over it or go around it. You know what to do. When life throws you a curve ball, don't say "Why me?" instead say "Try me."- Dwayne Johnson

Johnson is without a doubt one of the biggest stars of the present, and his star doesn't appear to be going out any time soon. He will play Black Adam in a feature film adaptation of the DC Comics superhero. After his poor origins, it appears like Johnson is in the best possible situation right now. Johnson, a former professional wrestler, has managed to become one of Hollywood's top box office draws. Furthermore, he was compensated handsomely for it; according to Celebrity Net Worth, his net worth is estimated to be around $400 million (and growing).

"Success isn't always about 'greatness'; it's about consistency. Consistent, hard work gains success. Success at anything will always come down to two things: focus and effort. And we control both. "- Dwayne Johnson

A forward for Juventus and the captain of Portugal's national team, Cristiano Ronaldo is a renowned Portuguese professional footballer. He is regarded by many as one of the finest players in the history of the sport and was crowned the greatest Portuguese player of all time by the Portuguese Football Federation. When Ronaldo transferred from Manchester United to Real Madrid in 2009 for a reported 94 million euros, he set a new record for the most expensive football player ever. Some people think of him as the best player in the world right now.

Ronaldo aka CR7 was raised mostly in a working-class area. His early years were mostly marked by difficulties. His father was a gardener who frequently drank too much and passed away in 2005 from renal problems. Because she supplied for her children and made sure of their financial security, Ronaldo's mother had a significant impact on his life. She supported the family by working as a chef and a maid. Ronaldo has always been enthusiastic about the beautiful game and has been training since he was very young. Ronaldo's quality was questioned several times, though. Even he occasionally had second thoughts. One such occurrence occurred at the beginning of the 2007–2008 season. Ronaldo received a three-match suspension after being sent off for a headbutt on Portsmouth defender Richard Hughes during Manchester United's second game of the year. He had a deep depression as a result of the harsh judgments of his skills. Ronaldo, though, was adamant about not giving in since he had a strong sense of confidence in his ability.

"We were quite poor, and I had nothing growing up. I didn't have any Christmas gifts or toys."- CR7

Ronaldo has emphasised that his unmatched success to date is the result of his enthusiasm and commitment to the game, not of some well-held secret. Persistence is essential for practically every new business. You must exert effort at the beginning. You can get the knowledge to learn from your past mistakes as you go along. By providing years of excellent service, you may grow your customer base. You become more assured that your concept will succeed. A feeling that will guide you to your goal is passion. I think that by pursuing your passion, you'll be one step closer to having a happy life. Just imagine a society in which everyone pursued their genuine calling by producing and acting accordingly.

He began playing for the Portugal squad at the age of just 17. He eventually became the best football player in the world because of his dedication. Because he put his life at risk when he was young to pursue his passion for football, he achieved a very high level of achievement. He now receives almost $108 million in total compensation. Ronaldo was awarded a €600.000 win bonus immediately following Real Madrid's UEFA Champions League victory in June of this year. Ronaldo said that he gave this substantial bonus to a good cause. As far as we are aware, he is the first Real Madrid player to have demonstrated this kind of compassion.

"I am not a perfectionist, but I like to feel that things are done well. More importantly than that, I feel an endless need to learn, to improve, to evolve, not only to please the coach and the fans, but also to feel satisfied with myself. It is my conviction that there are no limits to learning, and that it can never stop, no matter what our age." - CR7

Cristiano was identified as having a cardiac issue that, regrettably, caused his heart to beat rapidly even when he wasn't playing or jogging. He had to have heart surgery, which effectively addressed the issue, allowing him to run, practise, and concentrate on what was most crucial—achieving his ambition. However, he had challenges, setbacks, and disappointments just like every other person. But what made him the person he is today is his extraordinary ability to concentrate, work hard, and develop his talents every day. Cristiano Ronaldo has always had confidence in himself, regardless of how difficult the circumstances or the odds may have been. I consider myself the finest player in the world.

"I see football as an art form, and all players are artists." If you are a top artist, the last thing you would do is paint a picture that somebody else has already painted. " -CR7

Although your goals won't be attained right away, you will gain a competitive edge. Having a strong sense of attraction to something might help develop new values. You'll be able to view events from an insider's vantage point. If this helps you develop a better grasp of how to provide that value, it will be a significant benefit for you.

"I handled this job by taking a step back and considering the guiding principles and the desired impact since I am adamant that every difficult scenario offers a wealth of learning opportunities."

You may provide a solution using your enthusiasm for those who share your interest. Don't think that the only option to pursue your passion for art is to open an art studio and begin painting if you enjoy it. When we believe our passion will suddenly bring us fame and money, we are being deceived. But having a realistic timeframe helps with desire. Being able to stick means being enthusiastic. Being enthusiastic makes it possible to persevere longer than others. You will persist even when others give up because the path to achievement is too arduous and rocky.

"Small doses of willpower and determination are needed in our everyday lives at every step. there is always a choice that looks simpler and that will lead us away from our objective for every decision we make."

-Dr. Amit das

CHAPTER ELEVEN

Your Bigger Dreams Are Driven By Your Passion

"Never give up on what you really want to do. The person with big dreams is more powerful than the one with all the facts."- Albert Einstein

Keep dreaming until your dreams seem impossible to achieve.

Those who dare to dream frequently have a wider view of life and are able to transform the impossible into reality. Albert Einstein, a brilliant German physicist, is the author of this wise saying. He emphasised the value of being true to your goals, even if others may consider them to be "unrealistic." You will be able to notice how many chances are accessible that you might have previously overlooked when you strive higher and dream greater. Being more confident in yourself than ever before will also make it simpler for you to approach individuals and start a discussion with them.

> *"To start thinking beyond the box, consider your goals in life and whether they align with your passions."*

Additionally, you should learn as much as you can about the education and training needed for each job route so you can decide which one can provide you with the best chance at a successful future out of all those available. You need to stop worrying about what other people think of you and start thinking positively about yourself and your future. Stop worrying constantly about making mistakes, since doing so will make it more difficult for you to achieve great things in life.

> "*Aiming high and having great dreams forces you to push yourself in ways you never could have before. Your chances of success rise when you always consider the optimal outcome because you can prepare and think more strategically. By setting high standards for yourself, you inspire everyone around you to do the same.*"

When I mention Sundar Pichai, what comes to mind for you? The CEO of Google, who is Indian and headquartered in America, will be the obvious response. For additional information about the hip CEO of Google and Alphabet. Sundar Pichai, the CEO of Google, has joined the steadily expanding group of CEOs with Indian ancestry. Sundar Pichai's ascent to the top wasn't easy, but it was an excellent affirmation of India's position in the global technology sector. Since 2015, Google's CEO, Sundar Pichai, has been firmly in charge of the company. This straightforward CEO was born and raised in the southern region of India. Google CEO Sundar Pichai claimed that his father had to pay for his airfare to America in order to attend Stanford University, which cost him a year's income. He had never flown until that point, and he disappeared after that. He had a great deal of love for technology, and his open-mindedness encouraged him to succeed. He stated that since the beginning, computers have been his area of interest.

> "*He advised the kids to be impatient, optimistic, and open-minded and to believe that they had the capacity to change.*"

Being fearless entails having confidence in oneself and the notion that, with enough willpower, everything is possible. In order to improve your mood and accomplish more in life, you must also harness the power of positive thinking. There will be occasions when you feel disheartened because you are having trouble accomplishing your objectives. Because it can often seem worse when those close to you don't support your actions, it is said that "misery loves company."

However, try to focus on finding answers and assisting people who feel like they are trapped at a dead end rather than focusing on all the unpleasant aspects of life and how they make things tougher for you. By doing it this way, even if some people continue to think you're crazy for pursuing your aspirations despite what occurs, you won't care as long as you can assist others in doing the same.

"A person who is happy is not because everything is right in his life; he is happy because his attitude towards everything in his life is right." -Sundar Pichai

Pichai has made great strides since his origins in India. His time as CEO has been tremendously successful by most measures. In 2019, Alphabet generated $161.8 billion in sales, more than double the $74.9 billion the company brought in in 2015, the year Pichai was appointed CEO. Sundar Pichai was referred to as "the most powerful guy in mobile" by Bloomberg after he was chosen to lead the product teams for important Google services, including Android, Search, Maps, and more. The title was officially given to the Chennai-born engineer with a keen eye for product development by Google CEO Larry Page today. In 2022, Sundar Pichai's estimated net worth will be $1310 million (1.31 billion), or around Rs 10,215 crore. Every year, Sundar Pichai's net worth increases. The most popular app is Google, which provides immediate results in a matter of seconds.

"India has been, and has long been, an exporter of talent to tech companies." But it is in India that's now undergoing its own revolution. " -Sundar Pichai

A youngster born without a silver spoon in his mouth goes on to reach one of the most desired positions in the world via sheer hard effort, like in Pichai's narrative, which seems right out of a Bollywood film. Pichai intended to enrol in Stanford's PhD programme and pursue a career in academia, but he temporarily alarmed his parents by quitting to work as an engineer and product manager at Silicon Valley semiconductor manufacturer Applied Materials. Pichai joined Google on April 1, 2004, after earning his MBA from the Wharton School of Business in 2002 and working as a consultant for McKinsey & Company.

"You might fail a few times, but that's okay. You end up doing something worthwhile, from which you learn a great deal. "-Sundar Pichai

With all of that said, it is impossible to fathom this success without Sundar Pichai and his inventions, ground-breaking concepts, and—most importantly—desire to provide their users with the greatest possible experience. In one of his interviews with the New York Times, Pichai once revealed an intriguing tidbit about his humble upbringing: My life was quite simple compared to the world now, which was lovely.

"We shared a type of basic home with other renters. On the floor of the living room, we would sleep. When I was a child, there was a drought, and that caused us worry. I still need a bottle of water next to my bed to fall asleep. After seeing refrigerators in other homes, we eventually acquired one. It was significant."

Nothing short of inspirational can be said about the life of this former IIT graduate who is now the CEO of Google and the first Indian to hold that position. We all like the usual "rags to riches" tale, and there is something quite fulfilling about witnessing someone work hard and achieve success in life. Sundar Pichai, the CEO of Google, has led a life that is both inspirational and instructive.

"Let yourself feel insecure from time to time; it will help you grow as an individual. It is important to follow your dreams and heart. Do something that excites you."- Sundar Pichai

Only you can ultimately decide whether or not what you're doing is best for your life. If you don't enjoy what you do, it's likely that you won't put your heart into it as much, which will make it much tougher for you to succeed in life. To work with what comes naturally rather than forcing yourself out of fear, find a profession or career path that will enable you to spend the majority of your time having fun and utilising your natural abilities.

> "*Dream big, consider the best case scenario, work hard to achieve it, and then put up your best effort since this will lead to success. Aiming high and having a huge vision may be challenging, of course.*"

What purpose does setting modest objectives serve? When you can't get through to them, it might be demoralising. However, it gets simpler to stay going and achieve your goals if you establish bigger, more attainable goals and push yourself to succeed. When individuals have lofty goals for themselves and their lives, one of the biggest mistakes they make is attempting to tackle them alone. Even if you are exceptionally gifted, there are certain things that you simply cannot accomplish on your own.

Some would even advise against it. But it's necessary to think big and set lofty goals since doing so will make both your life and the lives of those around you more rewarding. You may always enhance your abilities by working with a coach or trainer, for instance, to keep one step ahead of the competition. Another alternative to lamenting what may have been done differently once it is too late is to learn from other people's errors.

"When we read the life stories of successful people, we learn a lot about how they have handled and overcame obstacles in their lives. Usually, it's easier to say than to do to follow your aspirations. You might start by finding some inspiration and motivation from others who have achieved their goals."- Dr. Amit Das

Never give up, says this son of a landless farmer who is now a billionaire and the owner of Thyrocare Technologies Ltd., the largest thyroid testing business in the world. One of the most clichéd things we've ever heard is probably that. But few people can maintain that level of commitment. Fortunately, there are others who will motivate you to press on. For instance, the son of a landless farmer from Coimbatore, who formerly struggled to eat twice daily, now controls Thyrocare Since setting off from the unremarkable village of Appanaickenpatti Pudur in Coimbatore, where he was born into a poor farming family and whose father couldn't afford to purchase him a pair of trousers or slippers, Dr. Arokiaswamy Velumani has travelled through some very challenging terrain.

According to Dr.Velumani, "My parents were not wealthy. They never had the money to treat me to a pair of chappals or pants. I was conceived at the base of the pyramid's ten segments. It wasn't simple. I am currently at the very top of the pyramid, though."

The country's medical diagnostic business had also been reinvented along the road by the bespectacled scientist. But because of his perseverance and hard work, Dr. Arokiaswamy Velumani, 65, is currently the Founder, Chairman, and Managing Director of Thyrocare Technologies, the biggest thyroid testing business in the world with 1,122 locations across India, Bangladesh, Nepal, and the Middle East! The world would be guided by our hearts first, and then by our knowledge to motivate others to take action .

Because of how unique each person is, the world is amazing. Let's be true to who we are. You risk losing sight of your actual purpose if you just see success in terms of monetary gain. I have found that those who are most alive do not depend on or are motivated by money. If you follow your passion, success will come to you. I've done a lot of studies on what makes something successful. The success of your life is influenced by a wide range of variables. We are unable to declare one to be more significant than another. You will undoubtedly be inspired by the numerous real-time personal success stories that can be found online. We constantly follow our passions.

Suresh Vazirani's made it so big from a Rs 1 lakh loan to a Rs 1000 crore company. Actually, it's not really a secret; more of an untold story. Once leader Jayaprakash Narayan was hospitalised with kidney failure, Suresh Vazirani became aware of the condition in Indian hospitals and made the choice to enter the healthcare profession. The importing dialysis equipment malfunctioned, and there was a critical patient in the hospital. As an electrical engineer, Suresh stepped in when the hospital was unable to provide assistance. He became aware of the challenges patients might face in these situations and the potential fatalities brought on by medical equipment technical failures.

So, at the age of 29, Suresh vazirani launched his first business, Transasia Biomedicals, with the intention of improving the Indian healthcare sector. Suresh Vazirani contributed about Rs 250, and his buddy lent him Rs 1 lakh. The business targets pathologists, lab technicians, clinicians, and technicians. In order to guarantee that Indian hospitals and clinics have access to the most modern technology, the primary goal is to offer items that are both inexpensive and made in India.

"Every two seconds, a Transasia gadget undergoes one test. On our apparatus, more than 150 billion blood tests are performed annually." -Suresh Vazirani, Founder, Chairman, and Managing Director of Transasia Biomedical Limited.

Motivation is fueled by passion. Having a passion makes you love the work you perform. Having motivation enables you to work efficiently. You must have the drive and responsibility to begin any assignment in order to finish it. One self-reflection question: Do you actually feel inspired to work? If the answer is yes, that's great; if the answer is no, you're not enthusiastic enough. If you are not passionate about what you do, it will just be a transitory life. You must develop a passion if you want to live over the long term. When you put your all into your job, it will undoubtedly help you accomplish anything in life. It will undoubtedly take some time, but your desire will help you maintain your patience till then.

There are several instances, like Mr. Mukesh Ambani, a great achiever in life because of his love for invention. He has the drive to be different and has to work very hard to get where he is in life. This will lead to big successes in life. We can accomplish a lot in life if we work for our objectives. But in order to keep it and improve the quality, we will constantly be devoted to our job. The devotion that comes from a job well done Last but not least, do what you love to do. Passion is an abstract concept. It inspires you to go against the grain and become enthused about the things you enjoy doing the most. You cannot be forced to do anything by anyone.

"If you're trying to create a company, it's like baking a cake. You have to have all the ingredients in the right proportion." —Elon Musk

Elon Musk has lofty goals and has accomplished them in his life. To achieve great things, you must have faith in your goals. It's only a matter of time before his vision of autonomous electric vehicles and passenger aircraft comes true. He did what seemed right. When he was 17 years old, he forced himself to live off $1 a day in order to follow his business drive. He dropped out of college to pursue his commercial interests, and he was successful. So, don't chase after money. If you follow your passion, money will come after you. People should pursue their passions, he said, with a valid point. That will make them happier than anything else. He is a leader with a vision.

"When you try different things, a lot of things aren't going to work, and that has got to be ok." Elon Musk

When he succeeds, he will go down in history as the person who started the entrepreneurial movement that other people followed. He is a driven businessman who knows how to break new ground. People are motivated by ambition to achieve the impossibly difficult. He goes off the beaten path. I always have optimism, but I'm practical," he said. I did not launch Tesla or SpaceX expecting to be extremely successful. just because I believed they needed to be done in any case.

He first had a number of failures during the rocket launch and gained knowledge from them. Even though he ran into several difficulties throughout the design and testing phases, he kept going. He said that failure is an option here. You are not inventing enough if things are not failing. Success has a price. A lot of sacrifice and effort are required for success. Due to a shortage of funding, Elon

Musk originally faced several difficulties. His entrepreneurial journey began with volatility, unpredictability, intricacy, and ambiguity.

"People can choose to be, not ordinary... yes, I think ordinary people can choose to be extraordinary."
-Elon Musk

He once faced bankruptcy when Tesla Motors was in a bad financial situation. He did, however, manage to survive by acting swiftly to fix things. You must go through hardships today in order to achieve success later in life. Trying to start a business is similar to making a cake. All the elements must be present in the proper ratio. Elon Musk is a model businessman who sets the standard for innovation throughout the world. By venturing outside the globe, he raised the bar for the populace. He will be remembered for his inventiveness and entrepreneurial endeavours. His ingenuity, entrepreneurship, and leadership are examples that other aspirational businesspeople should follow.

"Life can not just be about solving one miserable problem after another, that can't be the only thing," he says. "There need to be things that inspire you, that make you glad to wake up in the morning and be part of humanity."- Elon Musk

In conclusion, Elon Musk is a leader with a broad vision and a transformational mindset. For all generations, he serves as an inspiration.Numerous businesspeople and entrepreneurs have been inspired by Elon Musk's success. Elon Musk's journey of achievement includes a number of obstacles. But Elon always managed to fulfil his goals for the business he founded and bring forth a great conclusion.

"You want to wake up in the morning and think the future is going to be great, and that's what being a spacefaring civilization is all about," Musk said at the International Astronautical Congress in 2017. "It's about believing in the future and thinking that the future will be better than the past. And I can't think of anything more exciting than going out there and being among the stars."- Elon Musk

An industrialist and billionaire from India, Gautam Adani, The triumph of a man who had an ambitious idea and made it come true. After quitting college and declining to work in his father's textile company, Gautam Adani found employment as a diamond sorter in Mumbai in the 1980s. Adani began a brief career in diamond trading before becoming wealthy at age 20. In 1988, he finally launched a company that imports and exports goods. One such bright star in the Indian economy's sky is Mr. Gautam Adani. The Adani family is the richest, followed by the Ambani family. Unlike other corporate tycoons, however, Adani did not receive his money from his father. Instead, he made a concerted effort to alter his destiny.

When you examine Gautam Adani's success story, you can see how he employed hard work, business savvy, and a strong determination to create his ladder to success. A successful individual stands out from the crowd due to their foresight and ability to grasp opportunities. Gautam Adani is living proof of that. When the Indian economy opened the door to globalisation, he saw opportunities. He found it to be a blessing. He quickly expanded his business, using the circumstances to get access to the new market. As of January 4, 2022, Forbes estimates that Gautam Adani, the Chairperson of the Adani Group, has a net worth of a little more than US$80 billion. On November 24, 2021, Adani overtook Mukesh Ambani of RIL as the richest person in Asia with a net worth of $89.1 billion.

"You are either an extrovert or an introvert, and I am an introvert in that sense.I'm not a social person that wants to go to parties." -Gautam Adani

The 59-year-old is ranked # 24 on Forbes' 2021 Billionaires List and # 14 on Bloomberg's index of billionaires. It's crucial to comprehend an opportunity's potential. Adani has a vision. He understood the significance of ports in the development of an economy. Adani succeeded in gaining a stranglehold over the market because he saw the potential of commercial ports. He continues to own the most ports in India today. He continues to construct additional ports both domestically and overseas and is currently the largest port owner in India.

> *"He hadn't received advanced instruction from prestigious business colleges. He picked up business skills through witnessing trade practises, which helped him understand the value of supply and demand. He is a sharp observer who recognises potential areas of growth in demand and is a proponent of grabbing the moment when it presents itself."*

He is renowned for having unwavering principles and strong morals. Dealing with the government does not require you to pay a bribe, he said several times. The most renowned billionaires unquestionably originated in India, where family companies have been passed down from generation to generation. Over the past several years, the nation has gradually seen an increase in the number of billionaires. The Adani Group, a global corporation with its headquarters in Ahmedabad, India, was founded by Indian business mogul Gautam Adani.

"There are two turning points in my life. One in 1985, when the government relaxed import norms under an open general licence (OGL) for actual users. I began importing raw materials—polymers—and entered trading. The second turning point came in 1995, when we decided to get into the port sector, as part of the group's overall strategy to get into asset-building, "– Gautam Adani

With a net worth of 420 crore, Kanika Tekriwal, 33, emphasises the advantages of starting early and the vast opportunities available to young businesspeople today. The Kotak Private Banking Hurun Leading Wealthy Women list for 2021 has the youngest lady ever. Kanika Tekriwal, a Marwari woman born in Bhopal, founded India's first marketplace for private aircraft and helicopter charters after overcoming cancer. Her aviation company, JetSetGo, has grown to 10 private aircraft in the last few years. In order to offer services as a private jet and helicopter operator and aggregator, Kanika founded JetSetGo in 2012. JetSetGo is now India's first online private aviation charter marketplace.Kanika Tekriwal, founder and CEO of JetSetGo, demonstrated that nothing is impossible if you believe in yourself, despite her declining health and dominance of the airline sector.

She was diagnosed with cancer a few years ago, but she battled through it and beat it, and today she is the CEO of a business that has been compared to the Uber of the aviation sector. She is bringing good change to the heavily male-dominated aviation industry. She is a remarkable individual who made it onto the Forbes 30 under 30 Asia List for 2016.

"Dreams are not what you see in sleep, it is the thing which doesn't let you sleep." – A.P.J Abdul Kalam

We have a lot of things to do, but we don't enjoy them. Everything is based on an individual's needs. When we enter, we are delighted. When we take a tour with our friends and family, we are excited. With our loved one, we are content. When we do something very intriguing, we get excited. But have you ever considered how you feel when working? Do you actually feel content, ecstatic, or happy? Ideas are created out of passion. Being enthusiastic about something encourages the creation of fresh ideas. Because when we love someone, we always work to keep them shining, and this encourages us to think of new and inventive methods to improve the quality. These will spark the development of fresh concepts for solving that problem.

"When morning arrives, dreams aren't what you leave behind. They are what fills each and every minute of your life. The only thing standing between you and your dream's fulfilment are your willingness to try and your conviction that it is truly achievable."- Dr. Amit Das

CHAPTER TWELVE

Your Success Is Transient, Evanescent

"The real test is not whether you avoid this failure, because you won't. It's whether you let it harden or shame you into inaction, or whether you learn from it; whether you choose to persevere."
-Barack Obama

Success is never permanent; failures may last for a long time.

I advise individuals to make decisions with confidence, expect success, and promote their talents, which emphasises humility and an awareness of failure. Nearly everyone I spoke with in India downplayed their accomplishments. When I asked them to briefly describe their achievements, I was met with utter silence and blank looks. This wasn't because they didn't know or because their accomplishments were secret, but rather because they were uncomfortable answering such a basic icebreaker question. I had heard that they were modest about their achievements, but I never anticipated that humility to be so obvious. So let's take a trip down memory lane and examine things from a different angle! I view obstacles as stepping stones. A person's character and optimism are often put to the test by obstacles on their journey. Why are we more afraid of failure than success? Your negative ideas will gradually disappear if you form a successful habit, and you'll start to think that success will come through hard work and optimism.

"It's fine to celebrate success, but it is more important to heed the lessons of failure." -Bill Gates

Failure is okay because only then can you learn to get up and try again. As a result, without failure, success becomes boring. Neither success nor defeat are ever lasting. The more times you fail, the more methods you learn to avoid failing in a certain way. Anything you obtain without making an effort loses its worth. Everything you accomplish through a lot of effort and struggle is more valuable and precious. If coal is so accessible, what about diamonds? Instead, success is a deliberate decision to do things that you may not particularly enjoy doing when all the odds are against you, when it seems like nothing is working and there isn't a shred of hope: And you still cling to your fundamentals. Take immediate action!

"Just because you fail once, doesn't mean you're gonna fail at everything. Keep trying, hold on, and always, always, always believe in yourself, because if you don't, then who will ?" -Marilyn Monroe

Do you remember when Sushil Kumar, a Bihari native, made headlines by winning five crores on the fifth season of Kaun Banega Crorepati? Unfortunately, his life changed dramatically as a result of his victory, and he soon became bankrupt. 2015 and 2016 were the most difficult years for his life. He was at a loss for what to do. Sushil avidly participated in charitable work before realising it was all a joke. His connection with his wife was also damaged as a result.

> "*After KBC, I became a philanthropist hooked on "hidden gifts," attending over 100 events every month, Sushil Kumar stated.*"

Because of this, he was frequently the victim of fraud, which he discovered only after the funds had been sent. His relationship with his wife was gradually getting worse as a result of this. She would frequently claim that Sushil was unconcerned about the future and lacked the ability to distinguish between good and bad individuals. They used to argue a lot over this. People stopped inviting him to gatherings after he later disclosed to the public that he was insolvent. "And now, how did I end up bankrupt?" Sushil said. You'll think the narrative is a bit "filmy." One day, he was walking when a reporter from an English publication called. While things were going smoothly, he suddenly asked him a question that annoyed him, so he rambled that he had run out of money and was surviving on the milk from my two cows. Funny! But this is life.

"Success is always temporary. When all is said and one, the only thing you'll have left is your character."- Amitabh Bachchan

In the recent World Championship, Neeraj Chopra missed gold by a narrow margin to his co-contestant, Peter Grenada. When asked about his performance in the World Athletics Championships, Chopra expressed happiness and satisfaction with his accomplishments when asked about them. Chopra claimed that the competition at WAC 2022 was intense because all of the competing competitors had high averages.

"Never let failure into your heart; never let triumph into your mind. For those of us who feel defeated and devastated after each setback, this quote is crucial. You lose the opportunity to overcome failure if you allow yourself to be depressed for longer than a few days. On the other hand, future failures can be more difficult to handle if you let yourself develop an inflated ego following each triumph. Keep an attitude of humility and thankfulness for every triumph and setback you encounter."

In response to Chopra's comments on Peters' performance, the Grenada athlete did well to cross the 90-meter line and take home the gold medal. The hunger won't go away. Failure is most definitely not an option in today's culture, which is fixated on success and accomplishment. Failure and making mistakes are stigmatised or viewed as signs of human frailty. However, it will be hard to live and experience a successful and happy life if you try to do everything perfectly and are preoccupied with order and perfection. Accept your failure, whether it be one or many, since success is assured for the rest of your life if you have the appropriate mindset and are willing to learn from your mistakes.

"Although I am aware that people anticipated gold from me, things do go up and down. I'll keep working and training so that I can do even better the next time. I believe he can explain how Peter handled things better. Each athlete has their off-day. Peter's day was today. It was difficult for everyone. It is different for every athlete each and every time since he was unable to go to the Olympic finals. Comparing is not polite. I've picked up a lot from the circumstances today."- Neeraj Chopra

The Indian business magnate Vijay Mallya was the chairman of the conglomerate United Breweries Holdings and a multibillionaire. He was one of India's most well-known and influential business figures. Mallya founded Kingfisher Airlines in 2005 and served in the Rajya Sabha. He was renowned for leading a lavish lifestyle and was dubbed the "King of Good Times" in India. He possessed every material good a man could desire, including a private plane, an Airbus, many private residences, a fleet of high-end vehicles, and a private boat. He is a co-owner of the Formula One team Sahara Force India F1 and has designed a US$3,000 limited edition calendar. He was the owner of the IPL cricket franchise Royal Challenger Bangalore, valued at US$500 million, and he also paid US $250,000 to buy Tipu Sultan's sword. He also owned about 200 horses and 250 classic automobiles, among other things.

Currently, Kingfisher Airlines owes banks more than US$1 billion. He also made comments about being the face of all bank NPAs, pledging blue-chip securities, and paying an undetermined sum in court. In addition, he claimed that banks had NPAs of US$150 billion and that debtors owed considerably more than Kingfisher. And up to this point, Vijay Mallya has constantly denied any wrongdoing and said he is the victim of a media campaign. In order to prevent his reputation from being ruined, Vijay Mallya blamed the media in 2016 and attempted to explain why Kingfisher failed.

> *"Despite the slander, I have always led a respectable life and will keep doing so." Regarding the media's charges, all I can say is that I hope that sanity and common sense will prevail and that the truth won't be sacrificed to TRPs."*

So far, the government has recovered assets worth $3 billion from fugitives Mehul Choksi, Nirav Modi, and Vijay Mallya. While diamantaires Nirav Modi and Mehul Choksi, who are the primary defendants in the PNB loan fraud case, owe the bank over $2 billion, Vijay Mallya owes a consortium of banks nearly $ 1.5 billion. Included are Ramalinga Raju of Satyam Computers, Subrata Roy from the Netflix series, and famous jeweller Nirav Modi and his uncle Mehul Choksi. These rogue businessmen, "Bad Boy Billionaires"of India, they all ended up in jail owing to fraud claims and other reasons. Before India accused the fugitive diamond jeweller Nirav Modi of cheating Punjab National Bank alongside his uncle and pursued him all the way to London, he was worth US$1.8 billion. They were beyond wealthy, had the finest parties, and travelled in thc fanciest automobiles, planes, and yachts, but it all came to an abrupt stop when their shady business dealings were revealed.

> *"Success is ephemeral. Strive for long-term success. Over time, enduring businesses experience several increases. Create a business that will last for decades. You won't outlive that."*

According to Forbes in 2017, Nirav Modi, a celebrity jeweller, was valued at US$1.8 billion. The native of Gujarat, who founded Firestar Diamond, eventually established his own brand, Nirav Modi, with outlets springing up in cities like Mumbai, Hong Kong, London, and New York. They were beyond wealthy, had the finest parties, and travelled in the fanciest automobiles, planes, and yachts, but it all came to an abrupt stop when their shady business dealings were revealed. However, the disgraced diamond trader is now worth essentially nothing after being accused of committing one of India's worst financial scams in history. Since 2019, Modi has been incarcerated in the British jail, HMP Wandsworth.

When Modi left India, a massive manhunt was started, prompting the nation's officials to work with Interpol to capture the suspected fraudster. The Indian government wants Modi to return home, but his attorneys have been arguing against his extradition. After being formally detained in central London in 2020, he was given permission to challenge his extradition in August 2021 on the basis of mental health, with his legal team stating that he poses a suicide danger.

Mehul Choksi, the owner of the Gitanjani Group of jewellery stores, was detained in Dominica in May on suspicion of working with his nephew Nirav Modi to commit the aforementioned PNB theft. His arrest, however, was based on the allegation that he had entered the tiny Caribbean island without authorization from Antigua, where he has resided since 2017. The firm obtained a multimillion dollar agreement in 2007 to be the first Indian sponsor and official IT service provider of the 2010 and 2014 Fifa World Cups, and Ramalinga Raju, the company's founder, gained notoriety as a result. Raju resigned in 2009 after admitting to manipulating the company's records to the tune of US$1.5 billion. In a five-page letter to Satyam's board of directors in January of that year, Raju claimed that he had purposefully overstated the company's cash and bank balances and that, as his initial attempt to conceal the underperformance of the company grew more elaborate, it became "like riding a tiger, not knowing how to get off without being eaten."

Raju was given a seven-year prison term and a hefty fine on April 9, 2015, but a Hyderabad special court granted him bail after just one month. The court granted him parole since it was understood that it would take time to have a trial, according to The Hindu. Subrata Roy, who came from a low-income family and built an empire in banking, infrastructure, and housing, was once regarded as the model of the "rags to riches" story. The market watchdog in India then accused him of cheating investors. Roy has further been charged with breaking securities rules by the Securities and Exchange Board of India (SEBI).

> "*All people fail at certain instances in their lives, the only thing that makes them different is how they manage to stand up or how they choose to fail again.*"

India Today claims that Roy spent two years in prison before being granted freedom in 2016. In a plea to India's Supreme Court in November 2020, SEBI said that Roy owed US$8.43 billion and demanded that he either pay it or go back to prison. Roy maintains his notoriety as a prominent person in India despite the controversy and jail. A biopic of his life was going to be created, it was reported in June. Additionally, he appears in the popular Netflix series Bad Boy Billionaires: India, which debuted in 2020. The Sahara organisation issued a statement at the time describing the programme as "ill-motivated, false, and wrong."

"There comes a time in your life, when you walk away from all the drama and people who create it. You surround yourself with people who make you laugh. Forget the bad, and focus on the good. Love the people who treat you right, pray for the ones who don't. Life is too short to be anything but happy. Falling down is a part of life, getting back up is living." -José N. Harris

Everyone wants to live an amazing life, yet so few people actually do. Why is it so hard to find? The Values Factor reveals the straightforward yet incredibly potent formula for living a meaningful life. Spend some time with this book, and you'll be ready to live an extraordinary life for the rest of your days!

- Making wise choices when under stress is a common test of your mental toughness. It's crucial that you keep your ability to remain impartial and perform at the same level regardless of how you're feeling. When everything around you seems to be working against you, mental toughness allows you to keep going.

Learn to keep your problems in the appropriate perspective while remaining focused on your goals.

- There are constant pressures in life and business, as well as sporadic crises and unexpected turns. Make sure you have the tools necessary to handle the professional and personal problems you will inevitably encounter. To remain steadfast in the face of actual or future challenges, focus on the long-term results.
- A positive attitude toward failure includes complications, unforeseen consequences, and total failures. Reduce the harm, take the knowledge you've learned to heart, and go on. Refrain from ceding control to others. Your power is in your capacity to govern how you react to what is occurring in your actions and emotions, both of which you have control over.
- Success is sticking up for what you believe in. People that are successful never give up on what they really believe in. Though you've done your homework and know that your beliefs are the right ones for you, even if many others disagree with them, you shouldn't give up on them without a struggle.
- The standard shouldn't be lowered because of severe economic conditions or company challenges. Maintain your path of action and maintain high standards. A solid internal compass When you truly internalise your sense of direction, you never have to be concerned about being lost.
- Success is recognising small achievements. Take time to rejoice whenever a goal is attained or a challenge is conquered, no matter how small the accomplishment may seem. Every goal requires the completion of lesser targets first, so if you accomplish one, take some time to acknowledge the effort you put out.
- Success is acquiring new knowledge every day. Successful people are aware that learning is a lifelong process. Make time every day to chat to someone who holds a different opinion than your own, read an intriguing article on a subject you don't know much about, or watch a TED lecture on cutting-edge research.

Learning doesn't take long, so begin right away.

- Patience in the face of disappointment. Instead of giving up, see failure as a chance to learn and develop. Be willing to keep trying until you succeed. Constant optimism Even more so, when you come across negative people, maintain your cheerful attitude. Never pull yourself down; always elevate them. Don't let doubters spoil the purpose of what you're trying to do.
- Satisfaction Spend no time feeling jealous of someone else's home, marriage, family, vehicle, or career. Be thankful for what you do have instead. Instead of looking over your shoulder and being jealous of what someone else has, concentrate on what you have accomplished and what you want to do.
- Getting through fear is success. You feel invincible when you overcome a fear. It's definitely something to be proud of, even if it's just facing one minor fear each week. Greater concerns will take more time to conquer, yet any effort you make will be successful.
- If you can keep in mind that it's not about you, you can overcome obstacles and emerge stronger. Avoid taking things personally and wasting time asking, "Why me?" Instead, concentrate on what you can influence.
- Self-acceptance is a hit-or-miss proposition for everyone but the worst kind of waffler, so don't worry about satisfying others. Instead, put up a concerted effort to uphold moral principles and know what you believe in.
- If the ability to adapt to change really is the only constant in life, then learning to be flexible and adaptable will be among your most valuable skills. By strengthening your ability to handle difficult events, you can maintain resilience in the face of unfavourable forces.
- Your future is decided by your thoughts. Yes, by simply altering your thoughts, you may completely transform your life.
- Realizing how abundant your life is is a sign of success. Life is abundant with love, health, friends, and family. Understanding this is a crucial step in developing gratitude for what life has

provided you. If you can sense this, your journey to achievement has already begun.

- Don't push things to completion before they're ready or expect results right away. Consider everything as a work in progress; everything worthwhile requires effort and perseverance.
- Living a successful life involves a variety of factors. Some of the answers are straightforward, while others need a bit more effort. You are already far ahead of many other people on the road to success when you know what you need to accomplish in the areas of your life to become more successful. Discover these secrets and what you can do to make the road to success much simpler. The trip may be made much more pleasurable and less daunting by working with a life coach.
- Realize the consequences of "Your Action" and achieve your personal goals! While the majority of individuals only have three degrees of action—no action, retreat, and standard activity—if you're aiming for great goals, you shouldn't be content with the mundane. You need to comprehend the desirable high degree of action in order to advance.
- When it comes to establishing and achieving their objectives, it is the one thing that individuals frequently forget is self-discipline.
- All you have to do is be willing to jump in. The mark of a successful man is humility. Never assume that you are too smart to pick up new skills. You may suddenly lose everything. You'll be able to stand up and move again if you have humility.
- Talents for creating positive habits that will help you reach a higher degree of success more quickly and methods and pointers for developing the self-belief and self-confidence necessary to achieve the success you deserve!
- Success is understanding when you need to say no. Only a balanced existence can lead to success. Learning to say no is a necessary component of balance. Saying "no" does not suggest selfishness; rather, it only indicates that you have priorities and are aware of what requires your focus at any given moment.

- Words have the ability to either help or hurt us. Our choice of language affects more than just how we characterise our life experiences. It develops it. To put it another way, anything we persistently say will eventually become true. Recognize that every word we say and every idea we have has an impact on our biology. It could change us somewhat or drastically. Our words shape who we are. Whatever we keep repeating in our minds is essentially a practise run for who we will be.
- One of the keys to your long-term success is your attitude toward accepting responsibility for something as your own. Everyone who joins employment does so in the hopes of having a very successful career, but relatively few people really do.
- Your creative thinking may become more receptive to fresh opportunities for progress. It is a complex, interconnected path of discovery that may be understood in a number of different ways. The reader is encouraged to go off on a solitary excursion while effectively employing their intellect. Your willingness to reflect, pay attention, and investigate sets the only boundaries.
- The importance of having a solid strategy in place for your success and how the "key question approach" will make it a breeze to do so!

"Do not judge me by my successes, judge me by how many times I fell down and got back up again." -Nelson Mandela

References

- *Man's Search for Meaning, June , 2006 by Viktor E. Frankl.*
- *You Are a Badass: How to Stop Doubting Your Greatness and Start Living an Awesome Life, April, 2013 by Jen Sincero.*
- *Make Your Bed: Little Things That Can Change Your Life...And Maybe the World, April, 2017 by Admiral William H. McRaven.*
- *The Alchemist, 25th Anniversary: A Fable About Following Your Dream, April, 2014 by Paulo Coelho.*
- *Smarter Faster Better: The Transformative Power of Real Productivity, March, 2017 by Charles Duhigg.*
- *Tuesdays with Morrie: An Old Man, a Young Man, and Life's Greatest Lesson, 25th Anniversary Edition Kindle Edition, June, 2007 by Mitch Albom.*
- *The 5 Second Rule: Transform your Life, Work, and Confidence with Everyday Courage, February, 2017 by Mel Robbins.*
- *Hustle: The Power to Charge Your Life with Money, Meaning, and Momentum, September, 2016 by Neil Patel, Patrick Vlaskovits, and Jonas Koffler.*
- *Think and Grow Rich: The Landmark Bestseller Now Revised and Updated for the 21st Century (Think and Grow Rich Series), January, 2005 by Napoleon Hill , Arthur R. Pell.*
- *Now, Discover Your Strengths: The revolutionary Gallup program that shows you how to develop your unique talents and strengths, February, 2020 by Gallup.*
- *The Power of Positive Thinking, March, 2003 by Dr. Norman Vincent Peale.*
- *High-Hanging Fruit: Build Something Great by Going Where No One Else Will, July, 2016 by Mark Rampolla.*
- *Choose Yourself! June, 2013 by James Altucher, Dick Costolo.*
- *Mindset: The New Psychology of Success, December, 2007 by Carol S. Dweck.*

About The Author

Dr. Amit Das, is a renowned executive advisor, consultant, educationist, author, speaker and coach whose 25+ years of business experience provides high-impact, practical solutions that support his clients' leadership development and organisational transformations. Dr. Amit Das is recognised as an innovative, principled thought leader who combines intellectual rigor and discipline with an ability to translate theory into practice. His operational skills are coupled with a strategic ability to analyse, develop, and implement successful strategies for profitability, growth, and sustainability.

Dr. Amit Das has a successful track record in aligning learning and training solutions to key business strategy with a strong focus on flawless execution excellence to facilitate individual, business divisional, and organisational performance. He keeps relentless focus on measuring training impact and ROI, people capability building graphs, training process governance, performance coaching, and strategic thinking. These have been some of his key individual success traits. His core capabilities include performance coaching, designing training and development frameworks, psychometric assessment and analysis, competency framework development and assessments, content design and facilitation of soft skills and leadership programmes, Learning Management Systems, Learning Impact Measurement, Talent Analysis, and Performance Coaching and Counselling.

He has a Ph.D. and a Fellowship in strategic learning, along with his first class degrees in Human Resource Management, Marketing Management, International Business, and Corporate Laws from the top business schools in India. He is a certified Psychometric analyst, OD Interventionist, Human Psychologist, Lifecoach, Black Belt (LSS), Strategic Thinker, Talent Analyst, professional coach from the U.K. and behavioral coach from the U.S.A.

Printed by Libri Plureos GmbH in Hamburg, Germany